The Other Side of the Story

The Other Side of the Story

King of Kings Mohammad Reza PAHLAVI I

Ahmad KASVRAVI TABRIZI

ISBN : 1-4196-4341-X

To order additional copies, please contact us.
BookSurge, LLC
www.booksurge.com
1-866-308-6235
orders@booksurge.com

The Other Side of the Story

Chapters

In The Name of Ahura Mazda, In The Name of King of Kings

In The Name of United Eternal Iran.

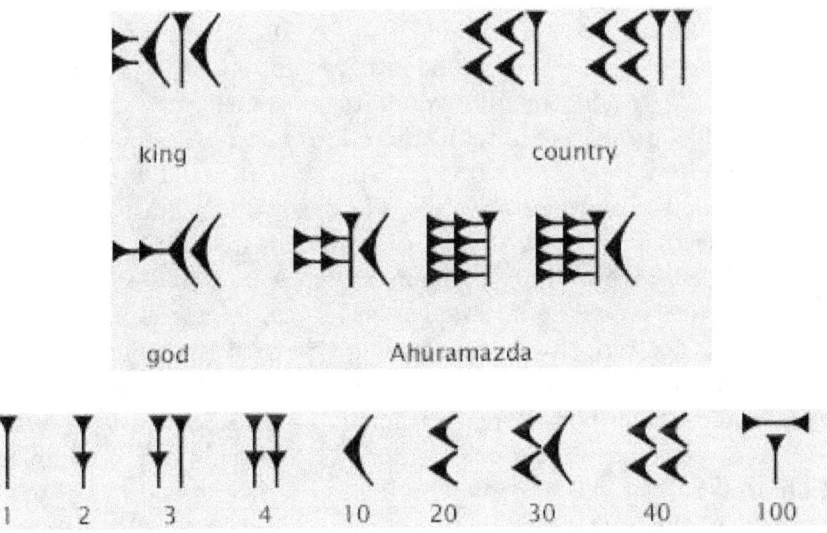

My God is Ahura Mazda {Wise Lord, according to Koran God has ninety-nine names}, my first Prophet is Zarathustra and my first faith Zoroastrian brought gift of monotheism, my first Holy Book is Avesta, my final goal is united eternal Iran, my spiritual leader is King of Kings Koroush {Cyrus}the Great, my commandments are written on Koroush Cylinder, my "*Nehjuo Belagheh*"{Islamic laws written by Imam Ali} is Education of Koroush {Cyrus}, my disciples are King of Kings Daruish, Khashayar {English is Xerxes and it means HE guides heroes}, Shapour, and Anushiravan "*Dadgar*"{just}, my "*Saoshyant*" {savior}King of Kings Reza PHALVI the Great, and King of Kings Mohammad Reza PAHLAVI First, my guardian angle is Crown Prince Reza Koroush PAHLAVI, my apostle is Ferdowsi, my Mecca is "*Takhteh Jamshed*"{Perspolise}, my Judas is

Salman Pars {Borzoob betrayed Persia to invader of Arab}, my *"Ashura"* {it means number nine in Arabic language, in this case, it is referred to Imam Hussein's martyrdom battle} is Battle of Qadissiyah, my Imam Hussein is King of Kings Yazdgerd Third, my Kaveh Ahenger is Ahmad BATEBI, my eternal *"Ahriman"* {evil}is Mullah, my *"Angra Mainyu"* is jealous and hungry Mullah who in every opportunity sought to destroy my pride land of Iran, my ideology is Iran, my cross is Faravahar, and Forever Persian Gulf.

This book is dedicated to mother land of Iran, as well as, His Majesty, King of Kings Mohammad Reza PAHLAVI military personnel who during early stage of bloodbath revolution of 2538/1979 paid ultimate price. In addition, those military personnel who were involved in *Nozheh* Coup and were fulfilling their duties as an Iranian patriot and loyal to their mother land of Iran and Iran's flag to save Iran from yoke of cold blooded murderer Mullahs. However, the military personnel were involved in the *Nozheh* Coup paid the ultimate price.

All the above military personnel from a foot soldier to a high ranking officer would be regarded as an Iranian Immortal Soldier, and this book is dedicated to all of them and written in their proud memory, so their surviving families know that there love one did not fall without cause and the fallen heroes are the Iranian Immortal Soldier. The heroes are not forgotten from anyone's memory, as a matter of fact, the Iranian Immortal Soldier will be remembering in our hearts and minds with respect and dignity forever.

Soon, a day will come in Iran that there will be a glorious monument which will be dedicate to the Iranian Immortal Soldier with their names on it, and a day to remember their ultimate sacrifice for Iran and Iranian people.

Viva United Eternal Iran.

Monarchy Date: 2565, Iran *Zamin* Date: 7028, and A.D: 2006.

Introduction:

I wanted to write a book with respect to 2538/1979 revolution because at the time of 2538 revolution I was a young person and could not comprehend fully what was happening on my immediate surrounding? I was in wonder, why people were killing SAVAKI in a street? Why people were killing military personnel or police officers on a bright day light? And why did King of Kings Mohammad Reza PAHLAVI refrain from ordering his soldiers to fire on mob {Oubash}? Until I attended university and took political philosophy courses, one of the political philosophy courses discussed Niccolo MACHIAVELLI political doctrines and I learned the MACHIAVELLI political doctrines. I engraved the MACHIAVELLI's political doctrines in my mind and found similarity between MACHIAVELLI political doctrines and the 2538 revolution in Iran.

The MACHIAVELLI political doctrines began to make sense to me how the Mullahs sparked the revolution in Iran, why the Mullahs murdered the military personnel and how the Mullahs established the Islamic Republic of Mullah in Iran, and why the clerics charged at left wing groups, and slaughter the left wing groups without faith and without mercy.

I became an eye witness to cruelty and malice of the Mullahs which encompass all aspects of Iranian people's life. I observed how the Mullahs with name of God lied to Iranian people, and how the Mullahs deceived Iranian people to rob their natural resources, how the Mullahs contemplated ideas to murder innocent Iranian people, how the Mullahs justified their crimes of sexually assaulting on Iranian females political prisoners before their executions in the name of God, how the Revolutionary Guards and *Besijs* apprehended an innocent Iranian lady {Banoo} and took her to their stations, and the Revolutionary Guards and *Besijs* treated an apprehended lady as their booty in their stations in the name of God. The Mullahs crimes are countless; the above mentioned crimes are merely the type of crimes which could be presented in this book {*Noskheh*}, and be presented with supporting evidences for future generation to remember how the Mullahs, *Sayyed* {*Sayyed* is an Arabic word which means Mr. in Iran *Sayyed* word is associated with children of Prophet Muhammad} or mosque imams {imam is an Arabic word which means a leader} destroyed land of Iran.

There was one more factor which was contemplating on me to write this book because when I was reading a book by Tom HOLLAND "Persian Fire": Published 2005, and another book by Barry STRAUSS "The Battle of Salamis": Published 2004. The above mentioned authors went through very hard time to write a well balance books on ancient Iran's historical events because there were insufficient books about Persia and Greek Wars from Iranian point of view because Iran was conquered three times by barbarians and all three times Iran's libraries were burned to ashes. First time, the Great Alexandra from Macedonia burned Iran's libraries to ashes, second time the Arab burned the Iran's libraries to ashes and last time was Changez Khan {from Mongol} burned Iran's libraries to ashes. Consequently, I had to write this book as an evidence for future authors in order to write a well balance book with respect to 2538 revolution in Iran. This book is the other side of the story of the King of Kings Mohammad Reza PAHLAVI that how Niccolo MACHIAVELLI political doctrines were executed in Iran which caused the King to be forced to self-exile.

Final note, I decided to use Ahmad KASRAVI TABRIZI as a PEN name for this book for two reasons. One reason that Mr. KASRAVI favored Constitutional Monarchy for Iran and last reason was because the Mullahs or children of Prophet Muhammad murdered Ahmad KASRAVI TABRIZI due to his constructive criticisms toward the Mullahs' Islam. Mr. KASRAVI was promoting and preaching true Islam and was encouraging people to refrain from the Mullahs' Islamic doctrines which were about superstition concepts. The Mullahs' source of income was about selling superstition ideas to people, and Mr. KASRAVI was not acting favorable toward the fanatic Mullahs in Iran. Therefore, the Mullahs assassinated Mr. KASRAVI in order to silent his moderate, logical and intellectual voice. In reality, the Mullahs failed to murder him and eradicating his ideas, the Mullahs by murdering KASRAVI has immortalized him and because of his books were remained as an instrument for Iranian people to educate themselves on how to approach God in a proper fashion and not in the Mullahs' fashion. Mr. KASRAVI stood assertively and firm against the Mullahs and challenged them firmly and others will follow his path and will challenge the Mullahs and not faith of Islam.

"Ahmad KASRAVI TABRIZI"

In 1890, Mr. Ahmad KASRAVI TABRIZI came to this world at city of Tabriz, Province of Azerbijon of Iran. KASRAVI was born in a patriarchy family who members were in field of profession of clerics. However, KASRAVI's father Hajee Mir Ghasem did not follow family tradition and did not become a clergyman. Mir Ghasem decided to work in a private sector as a professional businessman.

In 1897, Ahmad KASRAVI enrolled at school and studied Arabic language and learned Islamic doctrines {Share-at}. In 1902, when KASRAVI was twelve years old his father passed away. Consequently due to economic factor, he was forced to quit his school and attended labor market as a Persian rug maker. In 1910, KASRAVI decided not to continue his profession as a Persian rug maker and instead enrolled at a cleric school. In 1916, KASRAVI learned Arabic language very well and KASRAVI was admitted to one American school at city of Tabriz to teach Arabic language to students in return he was learning English language and plus he was making some earnings. In 1918, he joined Democratic Party movement. But then, in 1919, he stopped his political activities because former Soviet Union was providing financial and arsenal assistant to one Azeri separatist group, the Azeri separatist group assimilated communist ideology and wanted Province of Azerbijon to be separated from divine land of Iran. Plus the Azeri separatist group wanted Province of Azerbijon to become annex of the former Soviet Union territory and those Azeri-Iranians remained loyal to mother land of Iran would face firing squad of the Azeri communist separatist group.

In 1919, KASRAVI moved to capital city of Iran, Tehran and embarked in a field of judicial system as a judge in a courtroom. However, there were individuals that they could not get a long with him, and KASRAVI was forced to relinquish his position as a judge and commenced to work as a lawyer.

In 1927, Dr. Hortesfold CLASSI {apologizing for misspelling the professor's first name and last name, and writing his first name and last name in best of my ability} came to Iran and held lecture sessions on Pahlavi language and discussed how history of lion and sun reflect on Iranian culture. KASRAVI was thirsty for knowledge and did not hesitate a moment and KASRAVI attended Dr. CLASSI lecture sessions and was earning valuable lessons with regard to Iran's language and history.

KASRAVI continued to expand his intellectual horizon by doing his own independent research on area of Armenian language in Iran. He discovered that there were two types of Armenian languages in Iran, one language was old Armenian language which was called "Ghropar", and contemporary Armenian language was "Ash-khapor". KASRAVI continued his linguistic field and moved on Azeri language and came forward with evidence that the Azeri language was one branch or dialoged of old Persian language.

KASRAVI was an Iranian patriot and wanted to alter social and political dynamic of Iran. KASRAVI identified the Mullahs as a source of backwardness and corruption in Iran because the Mullahs in Iran preached and promoted superstition ideas to Iranian people. The number one clients of the Mullahs were businessmen at the emporium place who were dominated clients of the Mullahs bazaar. The clerics believed that a person could steal, cheat, deceive and commit any kind of immoral acts against another human being and God would forgive a sinner by simply donating portion of his/her money to a clergyman and/or paying a visit to Imam Hussein Shrine at city of Karbala which is located in today's Iraq, God would forgive the sinner. KASRAVI came to conclusion that Iran would not make a positive progress by having clerics who were encouraging people to commit immoral acts.

The businessmen at emporium were reliable source of income for the clerics. The businessmen in the emporium owned means of production and were controlling mode of production in Iran. The businessmen were causing intentional high inflation rate in Iran's market nationally by storing goods in their storages and causing shortage of supplies in Iran. Consequently, the price of goods would rise due to high demand; Iranian people were willing to pay to any demanded price in order to have good which was major reason for Iranian people to become poor and destitute. KASRAVI confronted the businessmen who were manipulating market equilibrium price and causing poverty in Iran. He wrote a book with name of "Haje-ha Anbar Dar Dini Cheh Mekonan?" it means "what are religious businessmen doing by storing goods?" KASRAVI exposed the Mullahs and the businessmen relation that how the businessmen were storing their products in their storages and causing high inflation rate in Iran which would lead to poverty in Iran. KASRAVI explained that how the businessmen deemed that God would forgive their sins by donating portion of their money to a clergyman and making a trip to Imam Hussein Shrine, God would forgive the businessmen of their sins. However, in Islam it is absolutely clear that anyone commits a sin; a person must ask his/her victim for forgiveness in person. There is no such a concept of medium to be involved in God and His creation.

The genealogy of the businessmen and the Mullahs relation goes back to seventeen century, under Safavid Monarchy dynasty, "Mulla Sadra locates the marketplace as a recruiting ground for mystics with exaggerating tendencies. He sees this public space of conversation as a socioeconomic threat: "[T]hese people's power is such that some craftsmen [san'atgaran] and artisans [pishahvaran] leave their jobs and follow them-what left of the common folk!" The pseudo-Ardabili speaks of merchants as targets of this group. "Some of them go to weak minded people's homes and voice their satanic whisper, and they go to the homes of the bazaariz, who know nothing of religion principles and sit with them and talk with them in order to fool them". [1] The Mullahs were fooling the businessmen at the emporium place because the businessmen motivated by greed and were not thinking critically with regard to their behavior.

The Mullahs were fooling anyone and their bazaar was also extended in physician field too. According to Mr. JAHED there is a pray for a headache, this pray has two sessions, in session one just to repeat chapter 112 of the Koran. The session two would be same as session one. [2] The Mullahs invented a pray for a stomach pain, a pray to become a wealthy person and so on. The Mullahs were not encouraging anyone to research in field of science and to find a cure for a headache or a stomach pain. Iran had Abu Ali Sin {Avicenna}, Abu Rehane Beroni and many more other physicians and scientists who contributed to the field of sciences. Iranian must perusal Avicenna books and to contribute to the field of medicine or studying Abu Rehane Beroni books and to contribute to mathematics.

The Mullahs were not encouraging people to make new discovery, or exploring new ideas, the Mullahs were promoting laziness and to become a Sufi was one element of laziness. The Sufi people would gather in one room, they span around themselves in a fast pace, and chanting certain words of Koran over and over, until the Sufi people would hallucinate and the Sufi people would assume that there was an act of divine or some kind of miracle occurred. Even some of the Sufis claimed that they could travel time and space without moving their physical body. The Sufis had long hair {oh yes like hippie}. KASRAVI rejected Sufism because Sufism was one source of inventing superstition in Iran. KASRAVI stated since a Sufi was able to do phenomena, then the Sufi should go to Europe and to report and to record his/her phenomena to European scientists or inviting European scientist to come to Iran and to learn from the Sufi how to perform phenomena.

KASRAVI was against culture of laziness and anything was associated with culture of laziness he would criticize that particular factor of laziness did not recognize Hafiz poems to have intellectual merit because the Hafiz poems did not motivate a person to take active role in their life. The Hafiz poems were sad and depressing. Such as, this particular poem by Hafiz; "1) When my Beloved the wine-cup in hand taketh, The market idols, disaster taketh. 2) In lamentation, at His feet, I have fallen, In the hope that me, by the hand, the Beloved taketh. 3) Like a fish, I have fallen into the sea, So that, me, by the hook, the Beloved taketh. 4) Every one, who beheld His eye said: "Where a Muhtasib, who the intoxicated taketh?" 5) Happy the heart of that one who, like Hafiz, A cup of the wine of Alast, taketh".[3]

KASRAVI encouraged Iranian people to take active role in shaping Iran's political dynamic, and particularly during Azerbijon dilemma he wrote a book with title of "what will happen to future of Iran's Azerbijon". He gave determining reasons that future of the Azerbijon was in hands of Iranian people and not in hands of the former Soviet Union, he asked Iranian people not to be passive but to be active and do all they could to keep Iran united. KASRAVI's books are available on line at this following web site http://www.kasravi.info/.

KASRAVI wanted to establish an Islamic sect with name of "*Pak Din*" clean believers. He wanted to eschew superstitions from religion, and plus he wanted to introduced Iranian people to core idea of Islam which was about unity among people as Koran was very clear about unity among people;" And verily this Brotherhood Of yours is a single Brotherhood. And I am your Lord And Cherisher: therefore Fear me (and no other). But people have cut off Their affair (of unity), Between them, into sects: Each party rejoices in that Which is with itself". [4]

The clerics and the businessmen were outraged at KASRAVI and wanted to eliminate KASRAVI forthwith. One representative of cleric from city of Qom and one cleric from city of Najaf from Iraq, with name of Navab Safavid issued a death decree {Mullahs issue a death decree for anyone, even for a child as young as nine years old, according to the Mullahs a nine years old lady is old enough to merry a man and to face legal system by herself, and one fourteen years old boy is considered to be legal, and responsible for his action. The Mullahs have neither sense of guilt conscience nor mind of reason} for KASRAVI at city of Najaf. Mullah Safavid came from city of Najaf to city of Tehran and met Mullah Hassan Talegani at mosque of Zahere Islam and mapped out how to murder KASRAVI.

In 1945, Mullah Safavid, and one terrorist person with name of Muhammad Khorshid, ambushed KASRAVI at intersection of Heshmatollah Al-Doleh at city of Tehran. KASRAVI sustained injuries and survived assassination.

The Mullahs were disappointed about attempted murder on KASRAVI's life. The Mullahs did not give-up on their hideous plan to take down monumental Iranian intellectual KASRAVI. The Mullahs used deceptions as the Mullahs were, are, and will be great deceptive people to carry murderer plan. The Mullahs wrote complained letter to the King of King Mohammad Reza PAHLAVI relentlessly, and accused KASRAVI for blasphemy. The King had to up-hold Islamic religion in Iran. As a result, KASRAVI was summoned to the court, and he was at the courthouse and had all his intention to resolve this blasphemy accusation peacefully. However, always and forever the Mullahs know one language which was, is, and will be violence.

In 1946, there was a second murder plan on KASRAVI's life, there were eight terrorists people from fanatic Muslim party of *"Fedayen"* {self-sacrifice} Islam attacked at him at the courthouse and murdered KASRAVI in cold blood. Once the eight perpetrators knew KASRAVI was finished, they shouted out loud God is Great {it is really funny always fanatic Muslim commit murder or some kind of immoral act and saying God is Great, as if God had approved their crime!} and left the courthouse. The terrorist were apprehended later one. However, the culprits did not face any kind of punishment because the Mullahs pleaded to the King to safe release the culprits. So the King did. At some point in future, the fanatic Muslim became bolder and assassinated one of the King's Prime Minister, His Excellency, Mansur Hassan Ali.

What lesson does KASRAVI's death give us? No one should ever compromise or sympathize with the Mullahs, they are children of Prophet Muhammad and cold blooded murderers, and in case anyone compromise or sympathize with the Mullahs, s/he will share same fate as Prime Minister, His Excellency, Mansur Hassan Ali did because the King was lenient toward clerics and allowed culprits to walk away from murder.

KASRAVI reasoned that there was only one type of a state which was suitable for Iran. KASRAVI focused on state of Constitutional Monarchy as a suitable state for Iran. He reasoned that the state of Constitutional Monarchy in Iran was acting as a medium for Iranian people to approach toward genuine democracy in Iran because the Constitutional Monarchy was governed by the Constitutional Laws which curtailed the Kings power. Furthermore, KASRAVI reasoned that Iran was a multicultural society and Constitutional Monarchy was an instrument to hold these mosaic societies of Iran together as one collective unit. He discussed how Iranian-Arabs in Province of Khozestan were naturalized to Iran, and further mentioned when there was some kind of invasion on Iran's territory by neighboring Arab nations; Iranian-Arabs who were naturalized to Iran would take stand against Arab aggressor, and other Provinces would join Iranian-Arabs cause and would defend Iran against Arab aggressor. As was the case during 1980-1988 Iran and Iraq war, when Iraq launched attack on Iran's soil, all Iranian-Arabs guarded Iran's territory and pushed out invaders out of Iran with the collaboration of other provinces.

KASRAVI was defending Iran and Iranian people against foreign forces of Britain and Russia and was encouraging Iranian people to become united force against foreign forces because in 1907, Britain and Russia signed a treaty with each other in order to divide Iran among themselves and each wanted to capture portion of Iran's territory. Britain wanted to capture south part of Iran for oil reason and Russia wanted to capture north part of Iran and eventually Russia wanted to make their rout to Persian Gulf as Peter the Great last Will mentioned that Russia must possess Persian Gulf. Thus, Britain and Russia were strangling Iran and as Morgan Shuster wrote a book with name of "The Strangling of Persia" in his book he discussed how Britain and Russia divided Iran. Britain and Russia failed to strangle Iran because of regional and internal political conflict. Britain was losing ground in Middle East because there was a creation of a new country with name of Iraq, and Russia was facing peasant revolution.

In Iran, King of Kings Reza PAHLAVI the Great used his influence and power in order to stop the strangling of Iran. The King moved Iran toward independence, and King of Kings Reza PAHLAVI the Great accomplished his ultimate goal which was to unify Iran's diverse culture and saving Iran from feudal war lords by establishing central government. King of Kings Mohammad Reza PAHLAVI First continued his father's agenda and used his political skills as well as his army and subdued Azeri communist separatist party. Thus, Province of Azerbijon remained as part of Iran's integral territory.

Britain and Russian's venom of disintegrating Iran still has remained. Today, there are some individuals who have affiliation with Azeri communist separatist party and residing in the United State of America and pretending to be Babak Khoramdin, Satar Khan or Bagher Khan who defended Iran against aggressors. One of the Azeri communist separatist member call himself "*Shoeravi*" which mean Russia, how naïve someone has to be to call himself Russia, even his name is not Azeri. They are other separatist groups. These separatist groups are making promises to their ethnic groups that how they are great leaders and their ethnic groups would be free from yoke of problems by becoming an independent country. What Iranian from any given ethnic groups need to know that problem is neither Iran nor their ethnicity but the Mullahs are the problem for their discomfort, unhappiness and good quality of life. These separatists are aiming toward their own personal political power at the expense of innocent people and as Machiavelli mentioned the only reason; "Factions or sects arise when a private citizen acquire excessive power, influence, or wealth through private means and employs it for private ends. The people he rallies to his support become partisans rather than citizens working toward common good and for public end. Political factions favor the interest of restricted groups of individuals and destroy the very bed rock of the polis, the sense of a shared community of values and goals accepted by all citizens. Factions promote the concentration of power and wealth, two major sources of political corruption, and rarely contribute to the general welfare of the state".[5] These separatists are strangling Iran and Iranian people and are not seeking common good of Iran, these Iran stranglers are seeking to have their own little countries, and once establish their own little kingdom, and they will kill anyone who speaks against their establishment as Pishevare did in city of Tabriz, and as Khomeini did in Iran.

Individual like Mr. Russia will claim that Azeri people were deprived to speak their Azeri language. He makes absurd statement because he wants to manipulate Iranian-Azeri people in order to achieve his goal. During reign of Safavid dynasty which was established by Azeri people and worked toward common good of Iran and Iranian people. At the time of Safavid dynasty; "Persian {language} itself had been the region's literary language following the Persianisation of Rum/Asia Minor from at least the thirteen century when Persian men of letters fled West in the face, especially, of Mongol incursions in the East. Jahan Shah Qaraquyunlu had composed poetry in Persian and patronized large numbers of poets and prose writers; even Ottoman rulers composed poetry in Persian".[6] One country needs to adopt one official language as a mean to communicate with other ethnic groups in a country. Additionally, Persian language was used in Middle East region by neighboring countries and the neighboring countries were communicating with one another in Persian language. Persian people did not impose their will upon other ethnic groups to use Persian language as a mean to communicate with one another. Otherwise, the Azeri Safavid Kings were brave and smart rulers and would deal accordingly toward Persian domination. Beside Safavid dynasty, there was Qajar dynasty which was established by Azeri people and used Persian language as a mean to communicate with other ethnic groups in Iran. Thus, Persian language was not a problem for Azeri people regardless of Monarchy Dynasty. These Russian lovers are having their own agenda and problems and want to cause social and political unrest in Iran forever, and not allowing Iranian people to become united in order to oust the Mullahs in Iran.

A prudent person thinks critically and examines other countries like China which could appear as a homogeneous society. However, China is not homogeneous society and it is as divers as Iran. China has five major ethnic groups, Han, Manchurian, Tibetan, Mosque, and Mongol with two major languages Cantonese and Mandarin. Also, there are sub cultures with their own identity and languages in China. And all different ethnic groups in China is living together peacefully as a collective unit and keeping China united. The other example is Canada which is Constitutional Monarchy and truly a diverse society. Canada has two official languages English and French and everyone is up-holding Canadian values.

The Iranian-Kurds played major role in shaping Iran's history and the Iranian-Kurds were in privilege position too according to Andrew J. NEWMAN; "sometimes before 1510 a Kurdish chieftain married yet another sister."[7] The Kurdish chieftain married Shah Tahmasb's sister. Therefore, Azeri, Kurds and all other ethnic groups created country of Iran, and Iranian people have to become a savvy person and not buy these sales men idea like Mr. Russia that Iranian-Azeri is deprived people.

Iranian people at broad have great responsibility to defend Iran, when a television station bring anyone separatist on their television programs, Iranian people must boycott that television station forever and to make a lesson out of that television station to other station that if any television station promotes disintegration of Iran will face boycott and will face bankruptcy. Iranian must adopt zero tolerance policy toward anyone who is strangling Iran. There are people like Ahmad BATEBI and many more people like him who is self-sacrificing his life for Iran. Therefore, Iranian out of respect to Iranian hero like Mr. BATEBI must boycott any television station which is promoting strangling of Iran period.

If King of Kings Mohammad Reza PAHLAVI First did not leave Iran, now All of Azerbijon territory would be re-united and all other territories, which were stolen from Iran during Qajar dynasty by Russian aggressor would join back mother land of Iran.

All in all, a prudent person would come to this natural conclusion that Iran would remain united by a king or a queen that monarchy is only factor to keep Iran in one piece otherwise Iran would be divided among ethnic groups because each ethnic tribe leader is seeking their own best interest and when Iran is divided among ethnic groups, each ethnic group has less power and less ability to do political maneuver on political stage and to resist world powers during crisis which is the case in Afghanistan. Today, Afghanistan is having a difficult time to remain as a united country because there are tribal leaders who do not want to work for central government because a tribal leader would lose his power and privilege. Having said Afghanistan is a defenseless country, it can be invaded by Russia at any time again because Russia must own the Persian Gulf. On the other hand, European nations joined to one another and their economic is flourishing and people's prosperity is enhancing.

"Execution of Niccolo MACHAIVELLI Political Doctrine in Iran"

According to Niccolo MACHIAVELLI "men gladly change their masters, thinking to better themselves; and this belief causes them to take arms against their ruler; but they fool themselves in this, since with experience they see that things have become worse".[8]

In 2522/1963 the Mullahs began to spark revolution in Iran when His Majesty, King of Kings Mohammad Reza PHALVI First implemented White Revolution in Iran. According to the King "the 1963 Teheran riots were inspired by an obscure individual who claimed to be a religious leader, Ruhollah Khomeini. It was certain, however, that he had secret dealings with foreign agents".[9]

In 2522/1963 the Mullahs sparked the revolution in Iran by leadership of Khomeini when His Majesty, King of Kings Mohammad Reza PAHLAVI ended feudalism in Iran totally, and commenced on his White Revolution policy in Iran. One aspect of the White Revolution policy effected serf and feudal lord and the Mullahs relation. The serfs were winner and feudal lords and clerics were winner too, but the feudal lords and clerics were greedy and did not want to share wealth with other member of the society. The feudal lords and clerics owned lands and they rejected the Kings White Revolution policy. The feudal lords and clerics wanted to resist the King's White Revolution policy and they took side with Tudeh Party {Iran's communist party}. The Tudeh Party was sworn nemesis of the King and did not like the King as a person, his position as a King of Iran and his policies, regardless how one policy or policies were formulated by the King which had intended to enhance social, economic and political equal opportunities in Iran. The Tudeh Party was a trouble maker for mother land of Iran and for Iranian people. The Tudeh Party had one goal on their agenda which was to hand over Iran to the former Soviet Union and Iran to become annex of the former Soviet Union Territory. Therefore, the Tudeh Party took side with feudal lords and clerics, and engaged in full-scale sabotages in Iran, and was undermining the central government's authority.

Indeed, Khomeini did have secret dealings with foreign agents. In 1963, when Khomeini caused turmoil in Iran, the King ordered Khomeini's arrest in order to create social order, social safety and security of Iranian people in Iran, and when Khomeini was at his home and was sleeping, Khomeini was apprehended by four secret police officers or known as SAVAK officers, the officers recovered foreign currencies, which were concealed under his pillow. The foreign currencies were U.S dollars, and British Pound.

In 1963, Khomeini HENDI {Khomeini's actual last name was HENDI which means he came from India} adopted a religious title as an Ayatollah. According to the King, "later the radio stations run by atheist émigrés belonging to the Tudeh Party accorded him the religious title of Ayatollah ("the sign of God") and praised him to the skies, although he was anything but divine inspired". [10] The Tudeh Party began to manipulate public religious sentiment and bestowed Khomeini with one title as the sign of God. Thus, Khomeini's authority became above and beyond the beloved King of Iran and above Constitutional Law of Iran. The title of Ayatollah meant that Khomeini was a messenger from God, and public must listen to Khomeini and disobey the King's order. The Tudeh Party was encouraging people to burn buildings, public transit buses, and any structure or property which were owned by the Monarchy Government. The Tudeh Party called Khomeini Ayatollah which means the sign of God; the Tudeh Party pretended that Khomeini was a religious person. However, Khomeini was not a religious person and was not the sign of God; he was a blasphemer and a rapist. {The rapist allegation against Khomeini will be discussing later on}. According to Islamic doctrine no one could associate anything with God, "the first doctrine is faith in the absolute unity of God, which is more than an intellectual assent to a proposition. The technical word for monotheism is *tawhid*, which means "making {God} one" by means of devotion and refusal to compromise on this point...He does not beget, nor is he begotten (sura 112)...suggest *shirk*, the "associating" of something with God, which is the one unforgivable sin in Islam". [11] Also every Muslim person's last right would be to state that there is no God but **One God**, and Prophet Muhammad Peace Upon him was last prophet of God. Further to the point of Khomeini's blasphemy charge, according to the Holy Book of

Koran chapter forty-three, section or verse fifteen "yet they attribute
To some of His servants A share with Him (In His godhead)! Truly is
man a blasphemous Ingrate avowed!"[12] {Fanatic Muslim people are not
showing any kind of reaction toward clerics who called themselves sign
of God, whereas, fanatic Muslim people showed reaction toward some
silly depicted Prophet Muhammad cartoons. These individuals so call
themselves true believer of Islam and holding a sign and stating about
murdering innocent people, and call themselves Muslim are just bunch
of punk who are looking for attention, and they are trouble makers}. The
Holy Book is crystal clear that there will be a day on earth that some
people will give themselves godhead name/s and to give a godhead name
is absolutely blasphemy. Beside Ayatollah title Khomeini also called
himself Ruhollah which means spirit of God. Once again, Khomeini
associated himself to God, and Khomeini would associate himself to
God at every occasion which was blasphemy. {Most likely, Khomeini
had high ambition and was competing for God occupation with the
God}. In 1963, Khomeini was apprehended and went to exile in Turkey
and resided in Iraq then France.

The Tudeh Party from beginning of their establishment in Iran
was a serious threat for Iran's national security; thirteen years prior
to 1963 riot at city of Tehran; "on February 4, 1949"[13] the Tudeh Party
orchestrated an assassination on the King's life and the King survived
the assassination. Consequently, the King disbanded the Tudeh Party
in order to create secure and stable Iran for investment and growth for
Iran and Iranian citizens.

In 2533/1974 the King moved Iran's oil toward independent and the
price of oil was adjusting itself according to equitable price equilibrium
properly. When the King was head of the OPEC, the price of oil was
in dispute with Western nations, the Western countries were not
please with new oil price equilibrium, the King relation commenced to
deteriorate with Western nations and wanted to oust the King from His
Throne. Immediately, the King began to face obstacles in his political
career and Khomeini was one of the King challenge.

The King could observe the calamity of His dynasty when "the
first signs of organized opposition to my rule came toward the end of
1976 from liberals, left-wingers, and people of wealth and power inside
of my country". [14] The liberals, left-wingers and wealthy people wanted

to do better for themselves and considered Khomeini as a force against the King. The liberals, left wingers and wealthy people were spreading rumors that Khomeini could speak three languages, English, French, and Arabic. Eventually, became clear that Khomeini could not speak of any above mentioned languages and even he could not speak Persian very well either. The liberals left wingers wealthy people and the Mullahs besmirched the King for stealing Iran's wealth. Their accusation had no prove, but their accusation caused Iranian people to become doubtful about the King's integrity.

In 2537/1978, there were more sparks in political air of Iran, the liberal, left wingers and wealthy people fully collaborated with Mullah Khomeini HENDI at full extend to oust the Monarchy Government and Democrat Administration of Jimmy CARTER manipulated naïve liberal, left wingers and wealthy people and the Democrat Administration of Jimmy CARTER was a real mastermind for the Mullahs to execute MACHAIVELLI political doctrines in Iran with medium of British Broadcasting Corporation {BBC}.

In first stage of revolution, Khomeini was using BBC and was sending messages to Iranian people inside of Iran, and asked the Iranian people to rebel against their King. Khomeini had one crucial message for rebellious Iranian that when the Iranian ousted their King and Khomeini returned to Iran he would provide free public transit, free oil to everyone, and free home electricity to everyone, given home to everyone at no charge, and no one would pay tax to government because it was against Islam to collect taxes and with plenty more freebees for the Iranian people, sky had limit, "Khomeini almost promises the Iranian people an Islamic paradise on earth, can be easily downloaded from the Internet. Yet even though every word the late ayatollah uttered in his lifetime has been reproduced in countless books and tapes, this speech at Behesht-e-Zahra has mysteriously disappeared from public archives in Iran".[15] Consequently, Khomeini was able to get public's attention because public wanted to better themselves, public wanted to become rich without merit and hard work. Furthermore, Khomeini accused His Majesty, King of Kings PAHLAVI of stealing from Iran's revenue. Khomeini did not have any kind of evidence to support his claim against the King that the King was stealing from Iran's revenue. Simply, Khomeini accused the King of thief in order to agitate public against their King. Additionally, Khomeini was poisoning the King relation with his citizens. The Iranian people were naïve and thought *Sayyed*

Khomeini one of Prophet Muhammad children was saying the truth. Khomeini lied and people bought his lie. Khomeini became bolder day by day and used BBC as an instrument to preach to rebellious people and asked the rebellious people to wear arm and attack at police, secret police, army personnel and barracks plus their families. The rebellious people were armed themselves against the Monarchy PAHLAVI dynasty and anything was associated with the Monarchy State and engaged in full scale of terrorist activities. The secret police asked all women who their husband was a police officer, secret police officer or in army to wear black head scarves in order to hide their identity in public areas for their own well being and safety. Khomeini caused social unrest and chaos in Iran.

The Humanitarian International Agencies played major role to bring down the PAHLAVI dynasty. According to King of Kings Mohammad Reza PAHLAVI; "I had already allowed the International Red Cross, the International Association of Jurist and Amnesty International to review our criminal justice system. I already asked for and accepted their comments, criticism and suggestions. We paid a good deal of attention to some of their recommendations. Needless to say the media reported the alleged abuses in great detail but paid little heed to the changes we made as a result of these missions".[16] The key point in above statement of the King was that International agencies and media manipulated Iranian and Westerners that there was an abuse in the executive and judicial bodies. The King mentioned that International agencies expressed concerned toward the executive system and judicial system and media paid little attention to changes. There is this valid question that who were prisoners?

The authority during reign of the King imprisoned terrorist people and some of the terrorist individuals were executed by order of a court; such as, a man with name of Red Rose {Ghole Soorkhee}. This man was a communist and believed Iran had to become part of the former Soviet Union Territory, he wanted to achieve his goal by murdering civilians, police officers, and sabotaging publicly own properties. During course of his trial a presiding honorable judge asked him if he would be release from incarceration, would he stop his terrorist activities? Red Rose responded by saying; "no" and he gave glamorous speech that he would continue his terrorist activities. He believed there was no reason to feel sorry for his victims, when he exploited a bomb in major road intersection and innocent people would die as a result of his terrorist action. He believed end would justify the meaning. As a result, the presiding honorable judge had no choice but to execute Red Rose in order to provide safety and security for Iranian people.

Examining Mujahedin-i Khalq {MKO} terrorist organization and some of their members were executed or imprisoned at the time of the King. The MKO was established in 1963 and their members were trained in terrorist field in Palestine. According to Michael RUBIN in his article title of "Monster of the Left: The Mujahedin al-Khalq" RUBIN highlighted MKO terrorist activists. RUBIN wrote, "a prison informant betrayed their plans to blow up a power station to disrupt the 1971 celebrations surrounding 2500th anniversary of Persian monarchy. An attempt to kidnap the Shah's nephew also failed." RUBIN went further and wrote that "in May 30 and 31, 1971, shortly before President Richard Nixon's state visit to Iran, the MKO launched a wave of bomb attacks which targeted the Iran-America Society, the U.S. Information Office, the Hotel International, Pepsi Cola, General Motors, and the Marine Oil Company. They failed to assassinate General Harold Price, head of the U.S. Military Mission in Iran…bombed the Jordan embassy to revenge King Hussein's September 1970 crackdown on their PLO patrons. In 1973, the MKO bombed the Pan-America Airlines building, Shell Oil, and Radio City Cinema in Tehran, and assassinated Colonel Lewis Hawkins, the deputy chief of the U.S. military mission".[17] The MKO profile was destructive for Iran and Iranian people and wanted to murder who was associated with the King and causing chaos in Iran. The authority, police or SAVAK {secret police} apprehended terrorist individuals and incarcerate them in order to establish social order in Iran. The authority had responsibility as well as accountability for safety and well being of Iranian citizens. The authority could not allow the terrorist individuals to terrorize Iranian citizens as well as foreign dignitaries. Interestingly, some member of MKO was able to cheat death sentence. In case of Masood RAJAVI was sentenced to death. He was able to avoid death sentence because of his brother, "launched an international clemency campaign".[18] The International agencies intentionally gave political prisoner status to terrorist individual and the King appeared on world political stage as if the King was suppressing his citizens. In addition, media portrayed the terrorist person as an activist and not a terrorist person. The media intentionally refrained to broadcast their terrorist activist in order to manipulate public opinion that the King reign was oppressive against his citizens. Without doubt, the MKO members were not peaceful activist, they were hardcore terrorist. Therefore, the Humanitarians International agencies and the Media created an oppressive image of the King against his own citizens that the King did not allow his citizens to enjoy basic Human Rights and was ruling Iran with Iron Fist. However, history must to record this evidence that the King did not rule Iran with Iron Fist. The King was treating his citizens with respect and dignity and the King obeyed the basic Human Rights. At the time of revolution, the King did not order his soldiers to fire at rebellious people. The King wanted to have a legitimate dynasty with people's consent. The King was not going to impose his will upon his citizens. The King did not authorize his army to open fire at rebellious people; the King ordered his soldiers to five bullets in their calibers, and had to aim at sky and fire in order to disperse rebellious people. In one case, at city of Tabriz one Azeri soldier was posted by U.S. consulate and eight rebellious circled him. The soldier told the rebellious in Azeri language and language was not a barrier for any of them that he had only five bullets in his rifle {Zh-3}. The rebellious people did not listen to the soldier plea, he was stabbed with knives several times to death and the rebellious people stole his rifle. There were more incidents such as above one in every city. Also some soldiers were stabbed and when taken to hospital doctors and nurse would kill the injured soldiers.

Disarming the King's Army:

The former Democrat President of United State of America Jimmy CARTER and his Administration were involved in accomplishment of 2538/1979 revolution in Iran. In 2538, the Democrat US Administration disarmed the King's army with help of General Robert Huyser by influencing one of Iran's top ranks General with name of Abbas GHARABAGHI. According to current available evidence that the US was involved in Iran's revolution with full intention to disarm the King's army, this evidence presented by Manouchehr GANJI former Minister of Education of Iran during reign of the King. In GANJI's book; "Defying the Iranian Revolution: From a Minister to the Shah to a Leader of Resistance" Published 2002. GANJI wrote; "Huyser started seeing General Gharabaghi, chairman of the Joint Chiefs of Staff, and other military commanders without the Shah's knowledge". [19] The General Robert Huyser was from the United State of America, and did not make a unilateral decision to come to Iran for a holiday by Caspian Sea or Persian Gulf resorts. Obviously, CARTER Administration instructed General Huyser to go to Iran and speak with the King's

Generals, and General GHARABAGHI as a top rank General who was a self-center person and was easily seduced by General Huyser to betray Iran. The General GHARABAGHI was a top rank General and convinced other Generals to remain neutral and not to make a coup at the time of absent of the King. As a matter of fact, several Generals did sign a paper among themselves to remain neutral during course of revolution, and when the King was departed from Iran.

Eventually, General Huyser brought to the King's attention, after one week from his trip in Iran. General Huyser was brought before His Majesty and when His Majesty observed General Huyser with General GHARABAGHI in his office, His Majesty was infuriated at General GHARABAGHI to bring General Huyser to His Majesty office after one week. The King knew that; "Huyser succeed in wining over my last chief of staff, General Ghara-Baghi, whose later behavior leads me to believe that he was a traitor". [20] General GHARABAGHI was sole General who did not face firing squad of the Mullahs. Assuming General Gharabaghi escaped the Mullahs firing squad with help of Mehdi BAZARGHAN {a lawyer and a revolutionary from National Front Party}. BAZARGHAN acted as General Gharabaghi's lawyer during course of revolutionary trials and Gharabaghi walked away unharm. Today, General Gharabaghi's fate is unknown to anyone and no one knows where he is now.

Once, General GHARABAGHI became a defector from the King's army, the British Broadcasting Corporation radio station and TV station aired Khomeini on their programs, and Khomeini would send messages in Iran and in one occasion Khomeini told the King's military personnel "do not you want to become your own master? Join people's force and **I (Khomeini) won't kill anyone**".[21] Khomeini asked the King's army personnel; do not you want to become your own master? Khomeini's message for the King's army was that the army personnel could do better when the King was ousted. Additionally, Khomeini was a *Sayyed* which meant that he was a descendant of Prophet Muhammad and there was a conventional wisdom that a *Sayyed* did not lie to anyone. In this case, Khomeini betrayed public trust and easily deceived military personnel by his background that he would not lie to anyone under any circumstance and the military personnel would be safe and secure from any kind of harms. When Khomeini took realm of power in Iran, Khomeini murdered and rampaged as many as military personnel he could do in cold blood.

On March 01st, 2006 Honorable Congressman Curt Weldon from United Stated of America appeared on National Iranian TV {NITV}. The Congressman wanted to reach to Iranian people who were residing in United State of America and was discussing the nuclear mullah issue on television. One viewer called the NITV and talked with the Honorable Weldon and the viewer blamed the CARTER Administration for ousting the Monarchy Government and helping Khomeini to establish his dictatorial kingdom in Iran. The Congressman responded; "I'm not Jimmy Carter but as a representative of part of the American People and a member of the US Congress, I do offer hereby my apology for what happened".[22]

King of Kings Mohammad Reza PAHLAVI wanted to stop bloodshed in Iran because the rebellious people under religious decree of Khomeini were murdering people with slightest suspicion that a person was a military personnel, police or SAVAK {secret police}. The King decided to leave Iran for a brief period. There was one political advisor with name of Sadighi who asked the King not to leave Iran, Mr. Sadighi believed if the King would leave Iran, the King's departure from Iran would be dire. However, the King did not listen to Mr. Sadighi and on Tuesday January 16th, 2538/1979 His Majesty, King of Kings Mohammad Reza PAHLAVI left Iran for a holiday. The King left Iran so rebellious people to stop bloodshed, and the King reluctantly relinquished responsibility as well as accountability of Iran in hands of Dr. Shapour BAKHTIAR's regency government. When the King was departing from Iran, the King last words were {as I was a witness to history when my own eyes observed and heard the King's words clearly}; "*Iran Iranistan kha had shoud*" what the King meant that "Iran will be a cemetery". History must to record that the King was absolutely, beyond a doubt was right when He said Iran will be a cemetery, and when on February 01st, 1979 Khomeini came back to Iran from France, Khomeini was escorted from Mehr Abad Airport to Tehran's cemetery, which was called Beheshteh {Beheshteh means paradise in Arabic language. Also paradise word was a Persian word} Zahra {it is an Arabic name for a girl}. Khomeini commenced repeating his promises that he was going to give freebees to proletarians, Khomeini preached that how he was going to distribute Iran's wealth to everyone, and then Khomeini lamented and besmirched the King for stealing Iran's wealth and filling the cemeteries with bodies! {Yes, if someone would sneeze, the liberal, left wingers and wealthy people would accuse the King for the sneeze, if someone would die of cardiac arrest, the King would be accused for the person to have a cardiac arrest and the King was besmirched for anything. Some readers may think, the above statements were written for sense of humor and as a joke, but that was the reality what I wrote.}

On January 16th, 1979 The King departed from Iran and there was a conventional wisdom among loyal Iranian to Iran that the moment the King was departed from Iran, the Central Intelligence Agency {C.I.A} would infect the King with some kind of health complication and would murder the King forthwith because if the King would be alive, His Majesty would defend Iran and once rebellious people came to their own conclusion natural that they made a mistake, they would revolt against the Mullahs. On Sunday July 27th, 1980 the King passed away and could not survive his cancer! God Bless the King of Kings Mohammad Reza PAHLAVI.

The King's Army Faced Khomeini's Firing Squad:

According to Niccolo MACHAIVELLI;"the prince who accomplished great deeds are those who have cared little for keeping their promises and who have known to manipulate the minds of men by shrewdness; and in the end they have surpassed those who laid their foundations upon honesty".[23]

On January 31st, 2538/1979 Khomeini departed from Neauphle-le-Chateau, France and on February 01st, 2538 Khomeini returned to Iran. When Khomeini was coming back to Iran, there was a conventional wisdom that Khomeini had one C.I.A gift with himself for the King's army. The C.I.A gift was Mr. Ibrahim YEZDI. The King defined YEZDI;" the famous advisor at Neauphle-le-Chateau-a peculiar figure who traveled with an American passport and became Bazargan's deputy and foreign minister".[24] Indeed, YEZDI was a peculiar person. He committed murder, and so far he has not brought before court and to question him.

When Khomeini was in an airplane on his way to Iran from France, {writing this segment, as a witness to history as I watched the Khomeini's arrival on television and heard everything clearly} there was a camera in the plane and showed an obscure character with name of Ibrahim YEZDI shared the airplane with Khomeini. Initially, YEZDI acted as a journalist in the airplane, the camera showed YEZDI approached Khomeini and hold his microphone on Khomeini's face and asked him; "how do you feel after fifteen years of exile coming back to Iran?" Khomeini told YEZDI; "nothing". Khomeini had no feeling whatsoever for coming back Iran nor did he have any feeling toward Iranian people because Khomeini's was a descendant of Arab invader of Persia. Khomeini had *Sayyed* title and Khomeini's descendant invaded Persia all the way to India to collect booty, and murdering people in the name of Islam. Khomeini did not care about Iran or Iranian people. Khomeini was a tool for Democrat U.S Administration to lower oil price, selling arsenal to Iran at high price, and Khomeini and other Mullahs were going to loot Iran's wealth in any shape or form as they could.

Once Khomeini arrived in Iran, he organized his mob enforcers or hooligans, the mob enforcers were divided in two paramilitary divisions one mob enforcer or hooligan was called Revolutionary Guard and another mob enforcer was called *Besij* {in Persian language hooligan was called "*Oobash*"}. Thug Khomeini became the muscle and figure of the revolution and Dr. Kiannouri {Tudeh Party Leader} advised Khomeini to apprehended the King army officers forthwith because of the danger of military coup d'etat which had to be discounted. Khomeini's hooligans apprehended the King's army officers without hesitation. The military personnel were imprisoned with false criminal charges; such as, "carrier/ spreading of corruption on earth" which was not part of criminal code, and the offence was not drafted and not legislated in any conventional parliament. The Mullahs self-invented the criminal offence of "carrier/ spreading of corruption on earth". Iranian never heard such an offence "carrier of corruption on earth".

The military personnel were imprisoned and any normal human would be panic for safety and well being of their love one and the military personnel were facing a bleak future. Khomeini had second gift for the King's army and Khomeini had one puppet with name of BANISADR. This Khomeini's puppet BANISADR played a crucial role in executing the King's army personnel. When the King's army personnel were held at "Rafah School"[25] without pending criminal charges, and without present of their lawyers, BANISADR would go to see these apprehended military personnel. BANISADR would comfort the apprehended military personnel at the Rafah School that Khomeini was the God's *Sayyed* and Khomeini would not execute anyone. After all, Khomeini promised to everyone on BBC radio that he would not execute anyone, and only reason to apprehend the person was for national security reason. The captive person would believe to BANISADR and would become calm. However, the captive military personnel were kept in darkness and they were going to face bitter reality of the children of Prophet Muhammad and puppet BANISADR. According to available evidence by Dr. Abbas MILANI in his book; "The Persian Sphinx: Amir Abbas Hoveyda: and the Riddle of the Iranian Revolution" Published 2000-2004. "For many of the prisoners, the ayatollah's words of comfort proved shockingly ephemeral. Less than a week after that visit, twenty-five of them, nearly all generals, were executed by firing squads on the rooftop of the Refah School. Indeed, the first round of executions that included four generals, Nematollah Nasiri, Reza Naji, Mehdi Rahimi {Honorable Immortal Iranian Soldier Mehdi RAHEMI at the time of his execution, he shouted out loud viva the King.}, and Manouchehr Khosrodad, took place only hours after the purported visit of assurance. Their trials had each lasted no more than a few minutes. They found guilty of "spreading corruption on earth".[26] This Khomeini's puppet BANISADR is walking freely in France and surviving families must put complains against BANISADR and apprehended him at once and to take him before International Court. The surviving families are sole complainers against BANISADR and must not allow him walk freely in France. BANISADR must be prosecuting for his crimes against Humanity. BANISADR was an accomplice for murdering the King's army.

Coming back at peculiar character Ibrahim YEZDI played an imperative role in Iran's post revolution. Initially he acted as a journalist for Khomeini on his trip back to Iran. Then, YEZDI began to act as a Crown Prosecutor for the King's military personnel "summery trials". YEZDI had no legal training whatsoever, he was a community college dropped out from the U.S. {Recently, YEZDI adopted title of doctoral for himself. Of course he has earned his doctoral on how to orchestra flagrant trials and how to murder innocent people. Once, he was finished with his assignment of murdering people, he returned to his master the U.S. and when YEZDI was residing in the U.S. for a brief period, the surviving victims were preparing criminal case against YEZDI. Once YEZDI came to conclusion that he was going to face serious criminal charges, and was about to be brought before court. He fled the U.S. and went back to Iran and he was force behind Reform Movement in Iran! Surprised do not be, Reform Movement was pioneered by former thugs in order to defuse the Student Movements in Iran} and YEZDI convicted military personnel for offences; such as, carrier/spreading of corruption on earth. There was a conventional wisdom among the King's army that the C.I.A prepared YEZDI a black list which contained names of military personnel that they had to murder them.

The Iranian Immortal Solider, Honorable General RAHEMI was not only victim of the Mullahs. The cruelty and malice of Mullahs encompassed on other military personnel too, who did not have legal representative in their Islamic Court of the Mullahs. These victims did not have legal representative nor were aware of their pending charges; "during this terrible month of March many other innocent people were "judged" and executed. The executed had no knowledge of accusation made against them; they had no time to prepare their defence; no lawyer; a trial behind closed door; anonymous judges-these were the innovations of so-called Islamic justice".[27] An accused person would be seated on a chair and one Mullah would state to the accused person his/her offences. At this very moment, the accuse person became aware that s/he was taken away from his beloved family due to corruptor of earth and many more unfound criminal charges. The accused person could not possibly to defend herself/himself. The accused person required to have sufficient time in order to gather evidences and presented his/her evidences to a neutral judge in order to defend her/him against pending charge/s. However, not in this case, the children of Prophet Muhammad laws were swift and the accused person was must to be murdered at once.

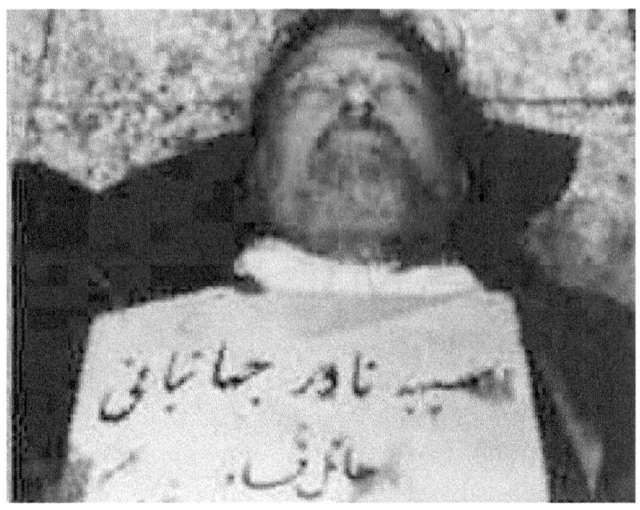

Iranian Immortal Soldier, Honorable General Nadir JAHANBANEE had one picture which indicated with the sign on his chest that he was convicted of offence of being "carrier of corruption". This Honorable General was loyal to Iran and the King and Khomeini one of children of Prophet Muhammad and Sign of God had promised to all the King's military personnel their safety, security and well being. Oh yes before forgetting this crucial point, Khameini one of children of Prophet Muhammad and Sign of God, the spiritual leader and supreme leader of the Mullahs had promised not to use nuclear bomb on Western nations.

Putting a real picture on cruelty and malice of the Mullahs. Madam Afschineh LATIFI's father was a Colonel during reign of His Majesty, King of Kings Mohammad Reza PAHLAVI First. And her father was apprehended by the hooligans during early stage of post revolution and the Colonel faced cruelty and malice of the Mullahs. Madam LATIFI wrote a book "*Even After All This Time: A Story of Love, Revolution, and Leaving Iran*": Published 2005 and described how the barbarian Mullahs children of Prophet Muhammad rampaged their life. Madam LATIFI described her account on how the savage hooligans apprehended her father, and how her poor mother was not aware where about her husband was, her mother was searching for her husband from one jail to another jail in order to locate her husband desperately, and when her mother was in a jail and was asking the hooligans where about her husband was the hooligans would use derogatory languages against her mother in order to ridicule her. Her mother remained persistence and determined to find her husband and eventually her mother found her husband at one of the Mullahs jail at city of Tehran. The Mullahs framed the Colonel with offence of murder and the Colonel's wife brought evidences before their Islamic Court to prove her husband was innocent of any offence and the Islamic Court with a Mullah as a judge one of children of Prophet Muhammad ignored her evidences and the Colonel was executed.

There is this question for all those international agencies that they were out crying at the King with respect to jail conditions in Iran. Where was the Amnesty International, Red Cross, or United Nation to defend LATIFI family from cruelty and malice of the Mullahs? They are busy with selling oil for food programs.

The execution of the military personnel was based on vengeance and had nothing to do with justice. In this particular time of execution, all left-wing parties and Iranian intellectuals were asking Khomeini to execute entire the King army and any one in any shape or form was associated with the King to face firing squad. The MKO leader Masood RAJAVI was one of front runner petitioner to Khomeini and was asking from Khomeini for Islamic Justice which was capital punishment for the entire King's army and anyone associated with the King. However, Khomeini had other plans for the King's army. Khomeini did not want to execute entire military personnel because Khomeini wanted to expand its Shiite Islamic State to other nations, particularly to Iraq.

The *Nozheh* Coup:

The King army was proud and loyal to mother land of Iran and Iran's flag. The army wanted to re-establish order in Iran and on several occasions mapped out a coup, and each time the coup failed. On July 09th, 1980, there was a failed *Nozheh* Coup which emerged on surface. There are two versions of the *Nozheh* Coup which are available on line. One version is prepared by http://www.sarafrazan.net/hamaseh.htm web site founder is Madam Shirin NESHAT whose father is one of Iranian Immortal Soldier, Honorable General Ali NESHAT and there is another article with name of "Anatomy of a coup" which provides slightly different version of the *Nozheh* Coup occurrence.

According to http://www.sarafrazan.net/hamaseh.htm web site the *Nozheh* Coup failed because there was one shady man with name of Ghorban-fer became aware of the Coup and learned about the details of the Coup, this shady man was able to associate with the Coup organizers. The shady man with name of Ghorban-fer reported the Coup to authority and a few hours prior to the Coup mission, all the Coup organizers were apprehended with help of MKO and other left-wing groups. Therefore, the Coup failed.

The Coup organizers were imprisoned and while they were in custody of the Mullahs they faced the most vicious, unusual, cruel, inhuman, and an animalistic nature of the Mullahs. There was one available testimony by Iranian Immortal Soldier, Honorable General Mehdiyoun's widow. When the Honorable General's widow went to city morgue to retreat her husband's lifeless body, she observed that her beloved "husband's left eyes was gouged out"[28], and leaving the eye socket empty. The body of this Iranian Immortal Soldier was riddle with bullets. The Honorable General's widow also observed signs of bruise and torture on the Honorable General's body. The cheap Mullahs demanded bullets money from the Honorable General Mehdiyoun's widow.

The Iranian Immortal Solider, Honorable General Mehdiyoun was belonged to Azeri cultural background; he remained loyal to Iran and sought to save Iran from savagery of the Mullahs. It appeared that the Honorable General Mehdiyoun failed in his Coup. However, the Honorable General did not fail in his Coup, as a matter of fact, the Honorable General gave other Iranian a valuable lesson so that the other Iranian to remain loyal to Iran, as the Honorable General told to every Iranian by his action that all Iranian have moral and nationalistic duties to be responsible as well as accountable to save Iran from yoke of the Mullahs. This Iranian Immortal Soldier, Honorable General Mehdiyoun resisted to last minute of his life as the savage Mullahs were demanding from him during course of integration that the Honorable General bow to the Mullahs, the Iranian Immortal Soldier Honorable General Mehdiyoun responded; "I will never kneel in front of you..."[29] and I will not kneel, you will not kneel and we will not kneel to the Mullahs, we will defy the Mullahs at every given opportunity, until Iran will be librated from yoke of the Mullahs period.

Everyone participated at *Nozheh* Coup were true Rustam because the *Nozheh* Coup participants did not wait for a prince or a king to save Iran from aggressor, the *Nozheh* Coup participants became like a Rustam and wanted to save Iran, the Coup organizers gave true meaning to Iran, Iran is a free land, and not belong to the medieval Mullahs.

The International Red Cross complained to the King that there was a problem in Iran's jail. Now when the Honorable General Mehdiyoun was tortured and murdered in cold blood. There was no sign of International Red Cross outcry to defend the Honorable General Mehdiyoun from brutality of the Mullahs. The International Red Cross and any other humanitarian international organizations are shields for the dictator states to fight with other nations and murdering innocent subjects.

Annihilation of Opposition Groups:

According to Niccolo MACHIAVELLI; "a new prince must always offend his new subjects with both his soldiers and other countless injuries that accompany his new conquest; thus, you have made enemies of all those you injured in occupying in the principality and you are unable to maintain as friends those who helped you to rise to power, since you cannot satisfy them in the way that they had supposed, nor can you use strong measure against them, for you are in debt; because, although one may have the most powerful of armies, <u>he always needs the support of the inhabitants to seize a province</u>".[30] Khomeini did not murder the entire the King's army because he needed the King army.

Prelude to Annihilating of Opposition Groups:

There was a conventional wisdom among the left wing groups or rebellious people that Mullah Khomeini and his entourage were not interest in politics. The rebellious presumed that Khomeini wanted to go to city of Qom {which was equivalent to Vatican} and to continue his theology studies. There was a cleric with name of Taleghani was spreading rumors around that the Islamic religion must not be mix with politics. However, Khomeini and his entourage were a cunning fox and had tasted power of politics, and became like a ruthless beast, a beast that tested human flash and blood and wanted more victims. Khomeini and his thug entourage were ruthless and anyone came between their political power ambition, Khomeini and his entourage eradicated the barrier from their root, the barrier was the left wing groups, {the liberals and wealthy people were on side of Khomeini} Khomeini opened a butcher shop and murdered as many as the left wing groups in Iran as if there was no tomorrow. Khomeini and his thus entourage tasted human flash and enjoyed the taste of human blood. Khomeini was a true Zahak as Ferdowsi wrote in his "*Shahnameh*" epic, how a ruthless ruler had sneaks on his shoulders and the sneaks were murdering young people and consuming flash and blood of their victims. Khomeini did not act any differently than Zahak.

The left wing groups and some individuals who called themselves intellectual presumed what the Mullahs were saying that the clerics were not interest in politics, it was true. According to Ms. Roya Hakakian, was one of revolutionary people in 1979, in her book "*Journey from the Land of No: A Girlhood Caught in Revolutionary Iran*": Published 2005. She thought that Khomeini was a simple leader who wanted the King to be overthrowing. Then, Khomeini would come back to Iran, and Khomeini would settle at city of Qom. Ms. HAKAKIAN thought that Khomeini would pursue his religious studies at city of Qom, and then the left-wing groups would establish their communist state or utopia. She was not expecting Khomeini to clash with the left wing groups because Khomeini as a representative of the cleric made alliance {in political term alliance is defined as convenient marriage} with the left wing groups and this alliance was called Marxist-Islamic which meant Marxist and Islamic doctrines were converged. Making Ms. HAKAKIAN thought more interesting from point view of Marshal BERMAN; "...the Shah of Iran. Then for a little while-rarely for more than a little while-the people may be able to take their development into their hands. If they are shrewd and fortunate, they will create and enact their own tragedies of development, simultaneously playing the Faustian and the Gretchen/Philemon-Bauci roles. If they are less than lucky, their belief moments of revolutionary action will lead only to new suffering that leads nowhere at all".[31]

According to Ms. HAKAKIAN's testimony at her own above book, she was a member of left-wing group. Hopefully, the left-wing groups had a chance to read Karl MARX and Frederick ENGLES book with name of; "The Communist Manifesto" the pioneers of communism were crystal clear that; "there are, besides, eternal truths, such as Freedom, Justice, etc..., that are common to all states of society. But communism abolishes eternal truths, it abolishes all religion, and all morality, instead of constituting them a new basis; <u>it therefore acts in contradiction to all past historical experience</u>".[32] Therefore, there was just matter of time that religious group to launch an attack on left wing groups with intention to annihilate the left-wing groups. If the clerics did not launch an attack on the left wing groups, the left wing groups would launch an attack on the clerics.

The Mullahs did deceive the left-wing groups by claiming that the Mullahs were Marxist-Islamist. The left-wing groups assumed because the Islamic doctrines encouraged people who have to share with people who do not have. The Islamic doctrines have guidelines for each individual to share his/her wealth with needy people as Christianity has the "Golden Rule". The Islamic doctrines instructed a person to pay *Zakat* {Arabic language for one fourth} which was one fourth of his/her income and *Khoms* {Arabic language for one fifth} which was one fifth of a household. The left wing groups assumed because the Islamic doctrines promoted sharing one's wealth, automatically the Islamic doctrines were compatible with communist ideology. However, the left-wing groups forgot to read Koran that God did favor class society, and God did not abolish class society.

The left-wing groups would shout slogan for establishment of a Theology State for Iran. Examining one of 2538/1979 revolutionary slogan:

"This is the national slogan: God, Qoran, Khomeini! People! Join us. Become martyrs in the path of righteousness! An Islamic Republic, Khomeini must be formed, Political prisoners, Khomeini says must be freed, The monarchist regime Khomeini says, must be abolished, This American Shah, Khomeini says, must be hanged! God is great, God is great, Khomeini is the leader, Khomeini is the leader! I will say it at every moment, I will say it under torture: "Death or Khomeini!" Iran is our country, Khomeini is our leader! A Moslem who remains silent Commits treason against the Qoran! This country will not survive Until the Shah is dead! Only one party: Hizbollah (Party of God) Only one leader: Ruhollah (Khomeini)! Our movement is Hosseini, Our leader is Khomeini!"[33]

At the time of revolution public were chanting above slogan and above slogan was crystal clear that Khomeini was the leader of the revolution, Mr. Sanjabi from National Front declared that Khomeini was the leader of the revolution force in Iran, and after overthrowing they PAHLAVI Monarchy dynasty, there was going to be a theology state, and the theology state was going to be established on the ground of Islamic Republic ingredients.

"The Unholy Alliance of Red and Black:"[34]

There was an inevitable bloodbath between Islamic fanatic religious group and the left wing groups. The left-wing groups political dynamic were not compatible with Islamic faith. The left wing groups were as aggressive and hostile as the Mullahs. The left-wing groups did not think that the Mullahs would out smart them, the left-wing groups deemed the Mullahs were gullible and naïve people and would be easy to suppress the Mullahs. In reality, the left wing groups were asking for trouble for post-revolution. The left wing groups were seeking window of opportunity in order to seize power in Iran since 1953 Coup.

According to King of Kings Mohammad Reza PAHLAVI; "Mossadegh's government demonstrated how such a red-black alliance could thrive without a clear understanding by the noncommunist members of its consequences. In early fifties, the Tudeh Party was merely biding its time, waiting for Mossadegh to oust me so that it in turn could safely eliminate him. We know this beyond question from documents found in Tudeh's offices after Mossadegh's sudden fall. The situation is no different today. The communists are waiting for Khomeini to lead my country into chaos, poverty, and despair before taking over."[35] The Tudeh Party was buying time and was allowing Khomeini HENDI to do what he wanted and then the Tudeh Party wanted to become a hero and save Iran from destruction. The Tudeh Party had to claim power by means of muscle and was not by means of democratic process.

Show Down On Annihilation of Opposition Groups:

On April 01st, 1980 public went to polling stations in order to decide for the type of political state for Iran. Prior to referendum there was not much of a debate. There was an absent of opposition parties in a parliament to debate details of a question, and how to approach to a question on a ballot.

There are three types of good state, one is republic, and two is constitutional monarchy and last is absolute monarchy. Therefore, public went to polling stations, and there was just one question for voters; do you agree with Islamic Republic of Iran? Yes or No. The outcome of this pre-engineered election was predetermining. Apparently, guess estimated, 98 percent of Iran's population voted for the Islamic Republic of Iran. What did happen to the left wing groups' utopia?

According to the Mullahs' propaganda, there was a landslide victory and the left wing groups felt left out of the political life. Khomeini tasted power, and power was too sweet for him to relinquish it. The left-wing groups wanted to taste power too and wanted to play politics.

According to Dr. Roy MOTTAEDEH in his book; "The Mantle of the Prophet: Religion and Politics in Iran." Published 1985 and 2005. MOTTAEDEH stated that "in 1981, the government decided to stop *Mojahedin* and other leftist groups from operating publicly, and these groups-believing that there was no more hope of constitutional opposition-had declared war on government...six thousand *Mojahedin* reportedly killed in shoot-outs or executed in prisons".[36]

Khomeini revealed his true face to the Iranian people and proved that he did not feel anything when he returned to Iran after fifteen years. Khomeini issued a decree that all left-wing groups to stop their political activities forthwith and the left wing groups were infidels, and must repent to Islam or face the Mullahs firing squad. The left-wing-groups did not embrace Khomeini's threat. The left-wing groups moved their political activities to next level which was to engage in terrorism. The left-wing groups targeted Mullahs in mosque, street or during Friday pray, and assassinated the Mullahs.

In summer of 1980, one Mullah, at city of Tabriz, died in hands of Mujahiden. The perpetrator was a young man, who approached the clergyman during Friday pray and killed the cleric. In his first attempt, he was unable to approach the clergyman. There was a second time attempt that he approached the clergyman or target, and asked the clergyman to get closer to him. The clergyman was not aware of the perpetrators' real intention and the clergyman allowed the perpetrator to approach him. The young man walked toward target calmly, the clergyman did not suspect anything from the perpetrator. The clergyman was surrounded by armed guards. Suddenly, the perpetrator hugged the clergyman and told the clergyman, "I am going to take you to paradise". The perpetrator had grenades with him, and the perpetrator pulled the safety pins. The armed guards rushed to save the Mullah from jaw of death. The armed guards commenced to hit the perpetrator with their rifle's bottom during short time frame. However, they all ran out of time.

The state of Mullah identified the perpetrator forthwith, and their hooligans rushed to perpetrator's house. The hooligans apprehended the perpetrator's brothers, sisters, mother, father, uncles from both side of families, and aunts from both side of families. They all faced firing squad of the Mullahs.

Khomeini revealed his true and pure dirty and animalistic nature when he issued a decree that all young females must be sexually assaulted prior of facing firing squad. According to Khomeini when a lady died virgin, the lady would go to paradise. Therefore, the hooligans had religious duties to ensure these females would not be admitted to

God's paradise. What if a lady lived for fifty years and died virgin and committed all kinds of sins. Is this lady still willed been allowed to enter garden of heaven? Who would believe to this kind of nonsense that if a girl dies virgin would go to paradise? Rapist people like Khomeini and his followers needed an excuse to rape ladies and from sociological point of view only one type of people commit sexual assault. An individual committed rape simply the culprit wanted to exercise his power on their victim. Khomeini wanted to exercise his power on his newly discovered subjects and to cause countless injuries in any shape or form and to impose his will on his subjects. Khomeini was in power position and causing state of fear in order to stop his subjects to participate in political life. Khomeini was in position to rape females and the victims' parents and sibling were powerless to defend honor of their family. Khomeini proved beyond reasonable a doubt that he could do anything to anyone at any time, and no one was in position to question Khomeini's crimes.

Massacre of 1988:

According to Machiavelli;" it is much safer to be feared than to be loved".[37]

On July 18th, 1988, Khomeini accepted United Nation Security Council Resolution 598 instituting cases fire between Iran and Iraq. Khomeini made peace with permanent President of Iraq Saddam HUSSIEN, as Khomeini called Saddam Hussein {*Yezed*, who killed third Shiite Imam Hussein, grandson of Prophet Muhammad at Karbla in today's Iraq, *Kafer*, which means infidel}. The eight years of war between Iran and Iraq was over. Khomeini and his hooligans feared the left wing groups because the left wing groups were in position to oust the Mullahs kingdom. Initially, the left wing groups were the terrorist force against the King to leave Iran, and brought the Mullahs to power. When, there was no more war, Iranian people were not defending Iran against aggressor, Iranian people would be thinking about Khomeini's promises that how he promised that people could better themselves by ousting the King, and their current condition was dire. Consequently, people's class conscience would rise, and the phenomena of class conscience would act as a cohesive factor among people. Once people were united, people would revolt against the Mullahs and oust the theology state.

Khomeini knew that the political prisoners were bad news for him because the political prisoners would organize themselves immediately, and would topple shamble Islamic Republic of Mullah at no time. Therefore, Khomeini relied on method of causing fear among his subjects one more time by executing the political prisoners. In summer of 1988 Khomeini and his hooligans executed 30,000 political prisoners. Temporarily, Khomeini secured his kingdom and defused any revolt for another ten years.

In summer of 1988, Khomeini issued a decree; "those who are in prisons throughout the country and remain steadfast in their support for the *Monafeqin* {infidel}, are waging war on God and are condemned to execution... Annihilate the enemies of Islam immediately. As regards the cases, use whichever criterion that speeds up the implementation of the [execution] verdict".[38]

In December 2000, one of prominent cleric with name of Hussein Ali MONTAZERI published his memoirs in which he revealed that, in 1988, MONTAZERI wrote a letter to Khomeini and told him about the poor judgment call on mass execution of the political prisoners and as not savvy approach toward the political prisoners; "at least order to spare women who have children and finally, the execution of several thousand prisoners in a few days will not have positive repercussions and will not be mistake-free... a large number of prisoners have been killed under torture by their interrogators...in some prisons of the Islamic Republic young girls are being raped...As a result of untruly torture, many prisoners have become deaf or paralyzed or afflicted with chronic disease".[39]

In 1989, the United Nation issued a document; "indeed, authorities of the Islamic Republic of Iran have always denied the existence of any political executions, but that does not contradict other subsequent statements which have confirmed that spies and terrorist have been executed (UN document A/44/153, ZB February 1989".[40]

In August 1988, one woman as a wife to a political prisoner and a mother of two children gave an interview to the Amnesty International at place of Jadeh Khavaran cemetery in Tehran, this cemetery was called by the hooligans as "Lanat-Abad" which means place of damned. The woman told Amnesty International; "Groups of bodies, some clothed, some in shrouds, had been buried in unmarked shallow graves in the section of the cemetery reserved for executed lefties political prisoners. The stench of the corps was appalling but I started digging with my hands because it was important for my two little children that I locate my husband's grave".[41]

The family of victims did not have right to hold funeral nor they were aware where about their loved one was buried in a plot. The left wing groups were gathering information about who was buried where and they could not confirm where the actual plots were. The left wing groups were doing their best to locate victim's body in order to inform their families. The Islamic Republic of Mullah simply would inform the families that their son, daughter, father or mother was executed, plus the hooligans on the phone would use derogatory comments toward decease family.

The Islamic Republic of Mullah was creative in their speedy trial. The political prisoners indeed had speedy trial. The political prisoners had such a speedy trial as the Mullah's judicial system ignored all rules of moral and law and created one commission and the left wing groups called the commission, the commission of death. This commission was the judge and the jury. This commission of death would call a political prisoner inside a room without a lawyer, without proper legal documents which were explaining reasons for his/her offence/s and consequences of conviction of offence/s, the political prisoners had no knowledge of what was going on, and what was intention of their questions. The commissioner would ask a political prisoner what was your political affiliation? If a political prisoner would mention that s/he was belong to the left-wing groups, the political prisoner would be taken away at once and s/he was finished. If a political prisoner was lucky and would say that s/he was belong to an infidel party. The commissioner would continue the flagrant trial and would ask next question that would s/he appear in television to condemn and expose the left wing groups? Obviously, if the political prisoner would say no, s/he would be taken away forthwith and face the firing squad. If the political prisoner said;" yes". The next question would be are you willing to go to war? The next question would be; are you willing to embarrass active member of left wing groups? If anyone was not answering the above mentioned question according to the commission of death, the political prisoners would face the firing squad.

According to one victim father's testimony, the hooligans would take the political prisoners to one grave yard sometimes from 02:00 hours to 04:00 hours. During 02:00 to 04:00 hours there were not people around and no one could become a witness the hooligans' cruelty. The hooligans would ask the political prisoners to dig the ground. Once, the political prisoners made his/her own ditch on the ground to some extend. The hooligans would open fire at them, the political prisoners would fall down due to bullets injuries and the political prisoners would not die right away because the bullets did not strike or mutilate vital organs; the hooligans would ignore *coup de grace* to their victims and intentionally the hooligans would bury the political prisoners alive.

The Islamic Republic of Mullah created a black list for the enemy of the Mullah and when a person name was entered in the black list. The whole family members were entered in the black list. As a result, the surviving family would lose their job at government, would not be allow entering at university, and/or would not be entitle to ration programs.

The above picture is an example of unholy alliance of Red and Black. There are grave plots of left wing groups without tomb stones. Flowers are spread on the ground.

During reign of King of Kings Mohammad Reza PAHLAVI citizens were not familiar and never heard a notion of mass grave yard and the notion of mass grave yard was an absurd idea because the King never killed anyone, except terrorist persons were found guilty in a court of law and convicted persons refused to rehabilitate himself. Therefore, an individual who was a terrorist would be executed in order to create a social order in Iran.

According to MACHIAVELLI, A Prince; "must know how to make good use of the nature of the beast, he should choose from among the beasts the fox and the lion; for the lion cannot defend itself from traps and the fox cannot protect itself from wolves".[42]

In 2541/1982 the children of Prophet Muhammad, the Mullahs legislated a sumptuary law which enforced women must to wear head scarf, male and female could not wear short pants, or short sleeves clothes. The Mullahs enforced their Islamic law by iron fist. Interestingly, according to Mullah Talegani during early stage of revolution he stated that Islamic dress code won't be enforced nor was compulsory. {What do you expect from children of Prophet Muhammad? They are liars [not Prophet Muhammad himself]}.

The Mullahs legislated sumptuary law because the Mullahs believed that a male and a female had these invisible rays and passing to each other which was source of corruption on earth. Therefore, the male and the female had to cover their body from each other, this dress code policy further banned anyone from wearing bright colors or wearing fragrance because an individual was wearing a bright color was accused of cultural diffusion. The Mullahs accused an individual of cultural diffusion because the Mullahs did not want Western values to be spread in Iran. However, the Mullahs forgot that Iranian would wear colorful clothes and wearing fragrances from ancient Persia time and colorful clothes and fragrances were part of Iranian culture, colorful clothes and fragrances had no relation with Western values.

The Mullahs' obsession with Iranian ladies sexuality is too deep {no seriously the Mullahs thought and ladies sexuality it is too deep}, and bringing forward one more example of the Mullahs' medieval idea and dehumanizing Iranian ladies occurred when the Mullahs had passed a law which banned Iranian ladies to ride bicycles. According to the fanatic Muslim Mullahs the Iranian ladies were riding bicycle and having sexual gratification, which was against the Islamic doctrines. Who would ever think of a bicycle seat and a lady? Just primitive and ruthless children of Prophet Muhammad would relate bicycle seat with a lady. As a matter of fact, the children of Muhammad were doing their own cultural diffusion on Iranian people by imposing their own Arab Bedouins culture on Iranian people, and this Arab Bedouins culture was not from Iranian-Arab descendant, this wild and animalistic culture was from Bedouins Tribe that invaded Iran.

According to Dr. Abd Al-Husain Zarrinkuh; "Muhammad's death in II/632 was followed in his successor Abu Baker's time by a crisis of an apostasy, the *Ridda*, which put both the religion and the government of Medina in jeopardy".[43] When Prophet died the Islamic doctrine that Muhammad preached were shaken by his death. "The new Islamic vigor was enough to achieve dominion over all the Arabian Peninsula".[44] Abu Bakr attacked at Iran during Sasanian Monarchy. This Monarchy had extensive battles with Romans and Iran's empire was stretch out which had direct effect on command of central government, and there was a religious conflict in Iran. The Zoroastrian faith had a cult with name of Mazdak which believed in socialism.

Abu Bakr needed to secure his own kingdom and needed to distract his people so he contemplated a plan to invade Iran and "Abu Bakr (II-13/632-4)...supplied the raiders against the borders of Sasanian Iran where Iranian, Nebatean and Arab peoples were mingling and living as neighbor".[45]

Abu Baker engaged in long military campaigns against Iran, he did not see the day that Iran was conquered, second caliph or spiritual leader Umar conquered Iran and after over one decade, there was one final battle between Arab and Iranian which was called Battle of Qadissiyah and Iran lost the battle to Arabs. All Iranians remember this point of history as Imam Ali with his children and one of his children with name of Hussein attacked at Iran and terrorized Iranians as our grand parents witness horrific wave of barbarian "on the day of Ctesiphon's capture, Iranians who saw Muslims crossing the [Tigris] river cried out,

"The devils have come. By God, we are not waging war against mortals. Rather, we are fighting none other than [evil] spirits".[46] Still to this day Iranians are defending Iran against clerics who are evil. The Arabs captured the city of Ctesiphon and burned libraries to ashes and said that Koran was sufficient and only book for source of knowledge and an absolute answer to all questions. There was a Persian Rug with name of four seasons which was made of all different kinds of precious jewels and silk. The invaders cut the Persian Rug into small pieces and ruined a national treasure. The Arab invaders took Iranian women as booty and slaved Iranian men and women. On the other hand, when Iran was governed by Monarchy states, the kings banned slavery, and laws of a captured nation would be respected.

When Umar and Ali ruled in Iran with Iron Fist, they implemented discriminatory laws against Iranian people. The second caliph with name of Umar implemented Covenant of 'Umar and Iranians beside of being *Ajam* {non-Arab} they were bounded by rule of "*dhimmis* were forbidden to build new houses of worshiping on new sites, but they could repair existing ones. They were not allowed to publicize their religion in order to attract new adherents, but they had freedom to maintain their own forms of worship and belief, passing them down from generation to generation. They were required to wear distinctive clothing, to treat Muslims with respect and deference, and to pay a poll tax, known as *Jiza*. The jizya was paid in lieu of the zakat, which the Muslims were required to pay. In addition, there was a land tax known as *kharaj*. The *dhimmis* could not bear arms, ride horse".[47]

All in all, the Mullahs wanted to take back modern and progressive Iran to the time of Muhammad the Mullahs brought back their discriminatory laws one more time and brought the dress-code policies and etiquettes which were alienated to Iranian people. Therefore, the Mullahs were doing cultural diffusion in Iran and were, are and will be enemy of Iran and Iranian people.

Briefly comparing similarity of two historical events in Iran, first Arab invasion of Iran occurred, when children of Prophet Muhammad took over Iran by use of brute and brutal force, Salman Pars {Borzoob} a Persian noble defected to enemy and collaborated with enemy on how to invade Iran, and Mazdak a socialist group as well as a religious cult allow Arab invaders to capture Iran, and 1979 revolution was a second Arab invasion of Iran. King of Kings Mohammad Reza PAHLAVI was a true Iranian Monarch, who was moving Iran toward great world civilization and as a principle *Takht Jamshed* {Persepolise} Gate of All Nations[48] was cherished for over twenty five thousand years of monarchy in Iran by

Iranian people. This time Arab Bedouins Tribe appeared as the Mullahs. Salman Pars appeared as the General Abbas GHARABAGHI, and the Mazdak appeared as the left-wing groups, they captured Iran, burned buildings, burned libraries, confiscated private property, murdered compatriot Iranians, murdering Baha'i faith group and taking women as their booty and forcing women in slavery. Yes, this ugly and sad history has repeated itself one more time, and now Iran more than ever needs heroes like "Yaqub Leys was the first Persian ruler to openly revolt against the Arabs. He brought much of Persia under his control and promoted the Persian language"[49] Babak KHORAMDIN, Hasan SBBAH, and many more Iranian heroes in order to save Iran from yoke of Arab Bedouins.

ﭼ

In 1999, university students embarked to organize themselves against repressive theology state. The students wanted to cherish basic Human Rights and legal rights; such as, freedom of expression, freedom of association, freedom of assembly, and many more freedoms which are recognized and practiced under Human Rights Declaration of the United Nation, and interestingly King of Kings Koroush {Cyrus} wrote first Human Rights Declaration. These university students' movement wanted to exercise Human Rights Declaration which was natural to them and was originated in Iran. The university students engaged in non-violence movement. In response, the Mullahs and their hooligans charged at the university dormitories at night and brutalized university students. The Mullahs and the hooligans murdered members of opposition groups, sexually assaulting females, and confiscating private property. The Mullahs knew that murdering people was not going to be a long term solution. The Mullahs invented Reform Movement in Iran. There were some hooligans like Asgharzadeh, or Mirdamad who attacked at the U.S. embassy during post revolution and took American hostages and Ibrahim YEZDI who murdered the King's army personnel were founder of the Reform Movement in Iran. The above individuals needed a clergyman in order to fill in the equation of deception of university students. The clergyman was Khatami and Khameini gave his blessing to Khatami to become president.

Khatami during his selection {it is a selection not election in Iran} campaign preached how he was Iran's Ghorbachoff {former Soviet Union President who caused communism to collapse} and wanted Iranian to cherish basic legal rights, to establish civil society, and dialogue of nations, and he wanted to open the door to U.S. {Khomeini labeled the U.S. as the Great Satan *Sheyton Bozorgh*}. Young university students were deceived by the Khatami's sweet talks. The university students asked their family members to cast their vote for Khatami at up-coming election and university students presumed that Khatami was McCoy. He was going to alter suppressive political dynamic of the theology state. Khatami did nothing to alter the suppressive political dynamic of the theology state. He was selected to office twice and the theology state violated Human Rights day after day.

The children of Prophet Muhammad, *Seyyed* or Mullahs are brain washed and always will suppress Iran's interest and Iranian people to eternal. The Mullahs are enemy of Iran and Iranian people. Kindly memorize this statement and teach your children, particularly to your daughters in order to have prosperous and free future.

The Mullahs are Arabs who their grandfathers invaded Iran. The Mullahs are brain washed people and are not naturalized to Iran, and care about their own kind, there was no wonder when Khomeini returned to Iran after fifteen years of exile he had no feelings to Iran and Iranian people. Khomeini cared about his own religious colleagues, and not a bit about Iran and Iranian people. In case of Khatami and many others Mullah who their grandfathers were Arab invaders of Iran, they are not naturalized to Iran and do not care about Iran and Iranian people, and all Mullahs are brained wash period.

The brain wash is a process which erases an identity of a person. And a person becomes part of a larger group. According to Sussan Babaie and Kathryn Babayan in their book "Slaves of The Shah: New Elite of Safavid Iran" when a slave was brought into a Safavid king's court "submission was to be absolute, for these slaves were fed, clothed, educated and given a new identity as Muslims by their master or mistress, the source of slave power. Slaves entering the abode of Islam (*dar al-Islam*) had been 'deadened' to society, and then through a process of conversation they metamorphosed into the *ghulaman-I khassa-yi- sharifa*, or slaves of the royal household as a distinct category in Safavid discourse". [50] The process of becoming a Mullah in Iran is not any different than how Safavid transformed a capture person to a loyal servant. There is a city with name of Qom in Iran and this city is same as Vatican of Rome. A young person who is a descendant of Prophet Muhammad would go to city of Qom and disassociated with his family for a long time. The young person read, studied all religious books, and associates with clerics and wears Arab invaders clothes because they want to be distinguish in a society and these Mullahs have mentality of time of Arab domination of Iran that Iranian people must to show respect and deference to them. The young cleric is not naturalized to Iran and Iranian culture but he has been brain washed totally and he does not see himself as an individual, he embraces a large community of cleric, and follows, promotes and protects beneficial collective ideas for cleric.

On December 2004, Mullah Khatami, brain washed like any other Mullahs, attended a farewell session at University of Tehran. He was confronted by angry students and demanded from him that what did happen to his promises? Khatami told students in front of Iran's national television point blank that he was selected {there is no election in Iran} as a president in order to defuse ticking bomb of revolution. Khatami was an instrument to pro long the Islamic Republic of Mullah. He had no agenda to alter political dynamic of theology state, he had no plan to create a civil-society and he had no plan to have dialogue with other nations.

Iranian people wake-up from this deep coma, how many times would you allow a cleric to cheat and rob your future? Taking a side with Crown Prince PAHLAVI Heir to Throne of Persia would be a wise and savvy decision in order to create a civil society, to have active political life, and dialogue with other nations peacefully.

Iranian people need to come down to a concrete conclusion that there is no children of Prophet Muhammad would ever feel sorry for Iranian people and with respect to Mullah MONTAZERI asked Khomeini not to kill all left wing groups and to forgive some of them {people called him *ghorbeh Nareh* because there was a cat from Pinocchio cartoon and the cat in the cartoon had funny accent which was resembling to MONTAZERI's accent} Mullah MONTAZER was following MACHIAVELLI political doctrine of "cruelty be well or badly used. Well used are those cruelties (if it is permitted to speak well of evil) that are carried out in a single stroke, done out of necessity to protect oneself, and are not continued but are instead converted into the greatest possible benefits for the subjects. Badly used are those cruelties which, although being few at the outset, grow with the passing of time instead of disappearing. Those who follow the first method can remedy their condition with God and with men as Agathocles did; the others cannot possibly survive". [51] Mullah MONTAZERI was asking Khomeini for one quick strike and not to drag his execution throughout entire summer of 1988. MONTAZERI could see that subjects' pain won't be vanish and would cause the Islamic Republic of Mullah to become unstable theology state because the Mullahs crossed the border line of fear and caused hate among their newly found subjects and hate never vanishes and perpetuated itself. The bottom line, "it cannot be called skill to kill one's fellow citizens, to betray friends, to be without faith, without mercy, without religion; by these means on can acquire power but nor glory". [52] The Mullahs have power but no glory. It requires Fortune and talent to balance a state on premise of power and glory in order to perpetuate a sovereign state peacefully.

On June 2005 Dr. Nezhad was running for presidency and Khatami's office revealed that Dr. Nezhad had "*Ahriman*" evil history. He was member of firing squad during post revolution. Obviously, he followed Khomeini's religious decree and raped female prisoners prior to their execution, and any imprisoned Iranian ladies were his booty. Therefore, he earned his doctoral in murdering innocent people.

According to Niccolo MACHIAVELLI; "Fortune is a woman, and it is necessary, in order to keep her down, to beat her and to struggle with her. And it is seen that she more often allows herself to be taken over by men who are impetuous than by those who make cold advance; and then, being a woman, she is always the friend of young men, for they are less cautious, more aggressive, and they command her with more audacity". [53]

In Iran's contemporary history, there were two Kings that they were building Iran and they were moving Iran toward independence and industrialization. First King was King of Kings Reza PAHLAVI the Great and last king was King of Kings Mohammad Reza PAHALVI First. Truly, they were saviors of Iran.

They saved Iran from hands of irresponsible Qajar dynasty because British and Russian were strangling Iran. Britain was looting Iran's oil and Russia was capturing Iranian territory by means of military invasion during Qajar dynasty and Reza PAHLAVI put stop on foreign nations from looting Iran and Iranian people.

The British and Russian did not like King of Kings Reza PAHLAVI the Great because he did not open Iran's door to foreigners to come in and loot Iran. The British and Russian did not like the whole idea, and decided to attack at Iran and forced King of Kings Reza PAHLAVI the Great on exile. King of Kings Mohammad Reza PAHLAVI became Constitutional Monarchy of Iran.

Incorporating Machiavelli concept of Fortune in PAHLAVI dynasty era as King of Kings Mohammad Reza PAHLAVI commenced to dance with this Fortune lady with Iranian traditional music and Fortunate was free and was not subject to any kind of cruelty. The melody was smooth and was heart pleasing for Iranian people. However, there was a scrooge with name of Jimmy CARTER. This scrooge was *Angra Mainyu* [evil] and wanted to make more money, he wanted to sell arsenal to Iran at high price and to buy oil at cheap price, the scrooge found puppets, BANISADR, Masood RAJAVI, Mehdi BAZARGAN and Emir Abbas ENTEZAM. The scrooge taught them that they could do better for themselves by ousting the King off the political stage. The puppets began to provoke citizens against their King and besmirched their King of crimes which had no merit.

The scrooge brought forward a young punk with name of Khomeini, who was shouting a song and was not making much of a sense. No one really understood Khomeini, but people decided to follow Khomeini, and Khomeini was shouting out loud, young people began to like Khomeini's out loud shouting. The King was a gentleman and did not want to cause a scene; he left the political stage for the puppets so that the puppets themselves to prove to Iranian people that the puppets were incompetent people to manage perplex international, regional and demotic politics in Iran. The time came and Khomeini and his followers rushed to the political stage and took over the political stage, and forced Fortune to cover herself up and not to expose her beauty to anyone in order to make her invisible to anyone.

The other puppets like BANISADR, Masood RAJAVI, BAZARGAN and ENTEZAM were smiling and cheering people to side with Khomeini. So, people thought Khomeini was making sense. BAZARGAN and ENTEZAM were wearing neck ties, and appeared to be professional people. BAZARGAN thought he could outsmart Khomeini. However, he was wrong; eventually, he was forced to quit the show business on political stage. Emir Abbas Entezam was trying his luck too and thought his boyish look and his killer smile will win him on the political arenas. ENTEZAM was wrong too. The scrooge did not like ENTEZAM very much, and decided to force ENTEZAM out of political stage permanently. ENTEZAM was chatting and flirting with American and Khomeini's hooligans mysteriously found a letter at U.S. Embassy with his name on it and the letter addressed him as "Dear". Khomeini's Islamic Court charged ENTEZAM with espionage and ENTEZAM went behind bar for twenty seven long years of torture and pain, good news still he is smiling {wow more than Nelson MANDELA}.

There came Khomeini's monkey Yasser Arafat, who promised to murder anyone for Khomeini. Khomeini did not like many people and on top of Khomeini's black list was Dr. Shapur BAKHTIAR. Arafat and his gangs tried twice on Dr. BAKHTIAR's life and eventually Arafat murdered Dr. BAKHTIAR. Khomeini was like a sugar daddy for Arafat, Khomeini was given free oil to Arafat, and Arafat was taking down targets for Khomeini.

Khomeini did not want to share his Fortune with anyone and decided to murder his competitors BANISADR and RAJAVI were first people on Khomeini's black list. BANISADR and RAJAVI were lucky and fled Iran. BANISADR and RAJAVI cried out loud that Khomeini high jacked their revolution. In reality, Khomeini did not high jack the revolution. The end product of the revolution was despotic state and bloodbath. The left wing groups were divided on two main categories from ideological view. One was Marxist-Leninist and other one was Maoism. When workers revolution accomplished in Russia, Lenin killed Tizar Monarchy family, killed opposition, isolated Russia from rest of the world and country was plunged down economically. Mao ousted the Monarchy State of China, isolated China from other nations and Mao published a red book and everyone must to read and follow the red book, and country was plunged down economically. Therefore, Khomeini did not high jack the revolution. Khomeini followed natural pattern of end product of unholy alliances, he eliminated other dictators and secured his religious kingdom. Khomeini was an aggressive person and was dancing with the Fortune lady and was not going to share his Fortune with anyone.

Fortune turned its back at the left wings and the left wings escaped Iran and those left wing groups who preached about communism and how wonderful was to live in an utopian society and a classless society and wanted Iran to become part of former Soviet Union territory. Individuals like Ms. HAKAKIAN and Dr. MILANI ran out of Iran and took refuge in the U.S. and did not go to former Soviet Union or China. The left wings embraced communist economic system, and the left wings would speak highly about utopian society and made passionate love with communist ideology. Ironically, they went to the U.S. which has adopted capitalist economic system which is opposite of communism and some how these individuals are contributors to capitalist mode of production by selling books, and maybe some of the left wings people own means of production and enjoying unpaid labor {profit}. On the other hand, the King's army personnel remained in Iran, loyal to motherland of Iran, and Iran's flag, they witnessed their comrades went to Khomeini's butcher shop and never return to their families, and did not flinch and did not flee Iran and defended Iran against Iraq invasion, and on several occasions had tried to save Iran from yoke of the Mullahs by doing military coups. There is this question for a reader to decide after reading above comparison between the left wing groups and the King's army experienced with the Mullahs. Who was loyal and true to Iran and Iranian people, the left wing groups or the King and His army personnel?

Now, the Fortune lady is exhausted of all this murdering and bloodbath, the Fortune lady is seeking a real prince, a prince could dance with Iranian traditional music and treat Her with respect and dignity that She deserves and has been ignored for too long, and to save this bored Fortune lady from yoke of the Arab Bodemenian Mullahs. This prince will save the Fortune lady as his grandfather, and his father did with help of Iranian people so the power and glory will be for Iranian people, anyone else save the Fortune lady, power and glory will be there and not for Iranian people.

"King of Kings Mohammad Reza PAHLAVI Was an Absolute Rule"

Iran is an ancient land; it has 7028 years of history, and 2565 years of monarchy with respect to 2006 A.D. Iran has faced numerous invaders with intention to annihilate Iran once for all; such as, Alexandra the Great from Macedonia, who burned Iran into ashes. However, Alexandra was not able to annihilate Iran totally. Iranian people re-claimed their mother land of Iran from the aggressor Alexandra.

In case of other invaders of pride land of Iran, Iranian people demonstrated great resilient against invaders the invaders were forced out of Iran totally or invaders were educated with Iranian knowledge and was naturalized to Iranian culture. In case of Arab Bodemenian invaders of Iran, they were forced out of Iran, but some settled in Iran and Mongol invaders assimilated to Iranian culture and they settled in today's Afghanistan.

Moving forward on Iran's history on fast track and arriving to the time of King of Kings Mohammad Reza PAHLAVI which is focal point of this paper, the King cherished Iran's twenty-five thousand year of history with Iran people and other nations, the King made magnificent speech to the dignitaries and in his speech he made ever lasting point that invaders of Iran never could annihilate Iran and Iran rose up from ashes. The King made a point that these foreign invaders caused Iranian people to have strong conviction toward their motherland of Iran and not let Iran to vanish in history.

PAHLAVI dynasty was established by Honorable General Reza Khan Mirpanj. Initially, Honorable General Reza Khan Mirpanj staged coup to save Iran from hands of Russia and Britannia. Honorable General Reza Khan Mirpanj merely could do the coup if he could have approval of Britannia. Additionally, Britain did not know that Honorable General Reza Khan Mirpanj had his own private agenda which was about moving Iran toward independence, and Britain was left on a crossroad, according to a British General Ironside who was involved in the coup and was acting behalf of British interest. General Ironside wrote in his diary; "I had to let the Cossacks go sometimes or other".[54] At the time, Iran did not have a central government which was well governed and the Russian force was invading Iranian territory from north part of Iran and Iranian separatist groups were outlaw bandits in each provinces and particularly *Peshevare* separatist group in Azerbijon Province was assisting the Russian force to invade Iran's Azerbijon. Moreover, the separatist groups in each province were looting weak and powerless Iranian people, killing innocent Iranians. Thus, the separatist groups brought further pain for Iranian people and instability to the central government.

The British could not defend Iran against the Russian force because there was turmoil between Ottoman Empire and the Britain in a matter of creation of Baghdad. The British came to conclusion that Iran was a lost cause because the Russian force was capturing Iranian territory at fast pace and there was not much of hope to defend Iran against such a strong force. The British wanted to minimize their loss. Therefore, General Ironside gave his blessing to a courageous man Honorable General Reza Khan Mirpanj to carry the coup. General Ironside gave his blessing to Honorable General Reza Khan Mirpanj because General Ironside calculated when Iran fell in hands of Russia; General Ironside would not be blame for loss of Iran to become part of Russian territory and loss of Persian Gulf to Russia. General Ironside approved the coup as long as the king Ahmad from Qajar dynasty would remain unharmed and the king would remain as a head of state of Iran. Honorable General Reza Khan Mirpanj promised not to harm the king. The British wanted an incompetent man as a head of state in Iran so the British could loot Iran's treasures and natural resources. At the time, king Ahmad from Qajar dynasty had no interest in Iran's politics, economics, or well being of Iranian people, he enjoyed chasing ladies in Europe and playing stock market, he left Iran's door open for invasion of Russia, and Russian force was capturing Iranian territory without any kind of retaliation. Iran was left in hands of an incompetent man with name of King Ahmad.

On February 21st, 1921 Honorable General Reza Khan Mirpanj staged a *coup d etat* in order to save Iran from the incompetent King

Ahmed from Qajar Monarchy dynasty because Russia was invading Iran and the king was doing absolutely nothing to defend Iran against aggressor. Honorable General Reza Khan Mirpanj achieved his coup and the King Ahmad remained as a head of state of Iran. Honorable General Reza Khan Mirpanj became Minister of War.

On December 12th, 1925 Honorable Reza Khan Mirpanj Minister of War was elected by the parliament of Iran by representatives of Iranian people, and Reza Khan Mirpanj became the King of Iran by consent of the parliament and new elected King established a legitimate Monarchy dynasty of PAHLAVI. The Qajar dynasty was ousted without bloodshed. The newly elected King rolled his sleeves up and commenced to build a nation of Iran. The King first and foremost agenda was to create one well governed central government in Iran for two reasons. One, the King wanted to establish a strong army in order to defend Iran against Russian's invading force. Last, the King wanted to defend Iran against the out law separatist groups.

The King pioneered Iran's railway from Persian Gulf to Caspian Sea because when the Russian military decided to invade Iran, the King could call for help, most likely British force, the King ordered to build secular public schools. Mullahs did not like the idea of public schools which was teaching secular ideas, the Mullahs were preaching to people if parents would send their children to public schools, their children, if a child was a girl would turn into a witchcraft, and a son would become a singer {at the time, Iran was a conservative society and was up tight}. The King abolished titles and any kind of privileges to anyone. Everyone had to work and earn money, and Iran's national treasure was closed down for free riders of society. The King introduced last name, again the Mullahs like Mullah Mossadr had problem with the King progressive plans. Reza Khan Mirpanj changed his last name to PAHLAVI.

King of Kings Reza PAHLAVI proved to be a brave and a shrewd ruler, some of the separatist out law decided not to wage war against Him and join the central government and those individual leaders were to ambition and wanted to have their own little country in mother land of Iran, the King capitulated them and placed them at city of Tehran under house arrest. PAHLAVI created a central government and Iran was kept in one piece. Most importantly, Reza PAHLAVI stopped Russian invasion and saved Iran to fall in hands of communism.

King of Kings Reza PAHLAVI relation with British began to deteriorate because the British wanted absolutely free oil from Iran and the British did not plan to pay Iranian people anything. The King's relation with Britain began to go further down hill, when King of Kings Reza PAHLAVI was making economical trade with Germany because Germany had advanced and high quality technological industry and Britain was not pleased with the King's decision to associate with Germany. Britain illustrated their disapproval to the King's decision to make economy trade with Germany. Britain attacked at a German cargo ship which was carrying shipment to Iran in order to build Iron facility at city of Isfehan. King of Kings Reza PAHLAVI the Great maintained his position with Germany.

During World War Two, King declared Iran's position as neutral country. However, Britain and Russia ignored Iran's position as a neutral country during World War Two, and they brought forward false accusation against His Majesty, King of Kings Reza PAHLAVI the Great as a pro-German. Therefore, Britain and Russia justified their act of invading Iran "British and Soviet forces attacked in the early hours of the morning of 25 August...the Iranian army collapsed within 48 hours and on 28 August Iran sued for an end to hostilities... Reza Shah was made abdicated in favor of his son on 16 September".[55] His Excellency, Prime Minister Forough was quick minded and made a savvy advised to His Majesty, King of Kings Reza PAHLAVI the Great to negotiate with the occupiers so that his son would become the king of Iran. His Majesty, King of Kings Reza PAHLAVI the Great instructed Britain and Russia that He would relinquish his responsibility as well as accountability toward Iran and Iranian people and in return the King expected Crown Prince Mohammad Reza PAHLAVI Heir to Iran's Throne to become the King of Iran. However, the British wanted to re-establish the Qajar dynasty in Iran by placing their own designated person as the new king of Iran. The British candidate could not speak one Persian word and the candidate could not communicate with Iranian people. Consequently, The Crown Prince Mohammad Reza PAHLAVI Heir to Persia Throne became the King of Iran. The British and the Russian were ruthless, they forced His Majesty, King of Kings Reza PAHLAVI on exile and His Majesty passed away at city of Johannesburg "on 26 July 1944".[56] The British did not stop their plan to destroy Iran, as a matter of fact, Britain embarked to "re-arm southern tribes to safe guard their interest in southern Iran"[57] while the southern tribes were armed, they would rebelled against the central government and would weaken the central government's authority.

King of Kings Mohammad Reza PAHLAVI First was a Constitutional Monarch, and Constitutional Law governed Iran. The King was complying with the parliament. There was only communication problem between the King and Prime Minister of Iran His Excellency Dr. Mohammad MOSSADIQ. His Excellency wanted to establish a republic system, and made a poor decision to curtail the King's position in the parliament. Thus, His Excellency invited the King for a battle. Therefore, the King has no choice but to issue a Royal Decree to relinquish His Excellency Dr. MOSSADIQ from his position as a Prime Minister of Iran by assistance of American. The Royal Decree was entrusted to Honorable Colonel NASIRI, who appeared at foot steps of His Excellency Dr. MOSSADIQ house and His Excellency was an intelligent man, he was no fool, when "Colonel Nasiri into action on August 15th".[58] 1953 and showed the King's Decree, His Excellency Dr. MOSSADIQ order to apprehended Colonel NASIRI at once because parliament was closed and the King's Decree had no effect. Now, the coup failed. "Roosevelt drove back to what he had begun calling his "battle station" at the embassy compound". [59] American began to distribute money {like a sugar daddy} around city of Tehran to mobs and caused up roar by angry mobs and the angry mobs attacked at His Excellency's house and one of the mob leader was a man with name of Shabon with his well known nickname brainless. Eventually, His Excellency gave-up to revolt of angry mobs and King of Kings Mohammad Reza PAHLAVI became an Absolute ruler of Iran.

King of Kings Reza PAHLAVI and King of Kings Mohammad Reza PAHLAVI wanted Iran to become a powerful and glorified nation and to regain its strength according to times of Achaemenid dynasty. On the other hand, the clerics or the Mullahs had their own diabolic plan for Iranian people, the clerics wanted to become heir to throne of Iran's monarchy from time of Safavid dynasty. Therefore, there was a conflict of leadership in Iran.

Fereydoun, HOVEYDA mentioned; "in 1970, almost every Iranian longed for a golden age, located in the past or in the future, but these golden ages were far from being same"[60] because Iran's political culture was divided on two different kinds of Monarchy dynasties. There were

Iranian citizens who wanted to move Iran toward Achaemenid dynasty and to have a Just King. On the other side of spectrum, the Mullahs wanted to move Iran toward Safavid dynasty which was established under Twelve Imams doctrine. In 1970, Iran's political culture which means;" values, beliefs, and attitudes that are the basis of political behavior. The political culture of a group is composed of the memory of important a historical events in the group's development and the symbols that crystallize the subjective meaning that their society has for them".[61] Thus, Iran's political culture was caught in two distinct dimensions, one distinct dimension was the Achaemenid dynasty and last distinct dimension was the Safavid dynasty. The Achaemenid dynasty and the Safavid dynasty each were single entity of their own distinct political culture of Iran and the Achaemenid did not converge with the Safavid in one collective unit.

The Mullahs and tycoon businessmen did not want the Achaemenid and the Safavid to converge. The Mullahs and tycoon businessmen {the Mullahs and tycoon businessmen relation was mentioned in chapter one how Ahmad KASRAVI explained the Mullahs were teaching the businessmen to commit sins and God would forgive the businessmen by donating portion of their income to clerics} preached about Islam being in danger if Iran moved toward secularism and the Achaemenid dynasty. The Achaemenid dynasty teaches Iranian citizens to become tolerant toward other ethnic groups, faith groups, freedom of thought and expression and teaches how to coexist with other ethnic groups. On the other hand, the Safavid dynasty was found on principle of Shiite Islam and with intention of expansion of Shiite sect of Islam to other regions and there was no toleration toward others.

In 558-530 BC, King of Kings Koroush {Cyrus} the Great was founder of Achaemenid Monarchy dynasty, and King of Kings Koroush was the founder father of Iran. The King was a spiritual person and there are two legacies from Him, one legacy was the Koroush Cylinder which is first Human Rights Declaration, and last legacy was Education of Koroush {Cyrus}. The Education of Koroush commands that a ruler must be a just ruler and establish a kingdom on foundation of benevolent. The King also trained a ruler how to protect his kingdom against an aggressor. {The Education of Koroush has more meaning and value than Imam Ali's Islamic doctrine book "Nahjo Balageh" the book is teaching someone how to lie, how to murder and how to lower social status of ladies in a society}. The six Achaemenid Kings name appeared in the

Holy Bible as just Kings. First, Koroush Persian name and Biblical name is Cyrus from Isaiah forty-five, Daniel, and Ezra one to three. Second king, Cambujieh Persian name, Biblical name is Ahasruerus Ezra four to six. Third king, Berooyeh Doroughi Persian name, Biblical name is Artaxerxes Ezra 4:7 to 23. Fourth king, Darryoosh Persian name and Biblical name is Daruis Ezra five, six. Fifth king, Khashayarshah {Greek called him Xerxes} Persian name, Biblical name is Ahasurerus Esther one to ten. And last king is Ardeshier Deraz Dast Persian name, Biblical name is Artaxerxes Ezra seven to ten and Nehemiah one to thirteen. Therefore, after providing valid evidence from the Holy Bible that the Persian Kings were just toward their citizens, and there was consensus among Iranian that a ruler must be just.

King Koroush name also appeared in the Holy Koran, according to Mullah Makarim al-Shirazi believed that there is a character mentioned at chapter eighteen verses eighty-three to ninety-eight with name of Dhul-Qarnayn, and the character Dhul-Qarnayn is Koroush the Great. Of course not all Mullahs are agreed with Mullah al-Shirazi. Once upon a time, during kingdom of Khomeini, there was a Mullah with name of Khalkhali and he had a nickname as a hanging judge. Mullah Khalkhali accused the King of Kings Koroush the Great for sexual deviant behavior and committed fornication. Mullah Khalkhali had no proved, he needed no prove, he was living testimony of god on earth and was one of children of Prophet Muhammad, so, naïve Iranian people believed him that the King was an immoral person and no one should ever think about their proud past. Truly, Mullahs are confusing people and cannot make their own mind. One thinks that King Koroush was a great leader and another Mullah thinks King Koroush was a deviant person. However, the Holy Bible is clear and crystal with respect to King Koroush and there is a Holy book with name of Avesta from religion of Zoroastrian and Iranian need to read Avesta and educate themselves about their own identity and culture, and not just to rely on Koran and Bible to educate themselves with respect to their own identity.

In 1501, Safi al-Din from city of Ardabil at Province of Azerbijon commenced to create a unified Iran, and Ismail became first king of Safavid dynasty. The Safavid dynasty had several key issues to confront Ottoman Empire. The Ottoman Empire was trying to capture Iran and was using Sunni sect as an element to manipulated Sunni Iranian against their ruler. Consequently, King of Kings Ismail ordered to establish a new distinct Iranian identity. King of Kings Ismail could not preach Zoroastrian faith to his citizens because his citizens were converted to Islam and anyone to reject Islam was constituted as an infidel and his/her religious condemnation sentence was death. King of Kings Ismail and his son Tahmasib Heir to Throne of Persia invented a new Shiite sect of Twelve Imams follower which was suiting Iran and Iranian people very well.

Iran became a distinct nation with respect to their surrounding nations. Dr. Rula Jurdi Abisaad in her book "Converting Persia: Religion and Power in the Safavid Empire" Published 2004.; "the monarch's gradual adaptation of a 'high' tradition of Shi'ism became one expression of their attempts, first, to convert the Persian aristocracy from 'Sunnism' to 'Shi'ism' and, second, to successfully thwart the formidable and expansionist Ottoman Empire". [62] The Safavid Kings used Twelve Imams follower Shiite sect as an instrument to reward their citizens "as earlier in the century many Tajiks, as already noted, retained discernible Sunni proclivities. Nominal profession of Twelver Shi'ism remained sufficient to secure employment at the central or provincial level over this period for those elites whose families, or who themselves, had served the region's earlier non-Shi'i political establishment". [63]

The Twelve Imams Shiite sect had Iranian roots as Dr. Babayan explained with regard to Twelve Imams Shiite sect; "Mazdeans divided human history into three millennia "ushered in successively by Zarathustra and first two World Savior." The Mazdean third savior, Saoshyant, is here equated with the Muslim apocalyptic world conqueror of the auspicious conjunction as well as the Mehdi and the Persian sun...the twelve solar months, twelve Persian dots, and twelve Imams are identical: "they are the Persian soul and the manifestation of which is the sun, and the manifestation of twelve is from the sun. There is a circularly in Nuqtavi logic, for they claim that "the sun has twelve houses and the twelfth Imam implies him [Mahmud], who is the manifestation of p پ, ch چ, zh ژ, g چ {actually letter g in Persian language has one dot. There is a letter geh گ in Persian language this letter geh distinguishes a Persian word from an Arabic word which is integrated in Persian language}". [64] King of Kings Ismail could not preach and promoted His new invented Shiite sect of Twelve Imams by himself, he needed "clerics who could wed Shi'ism to Savaid statehood and provide stability and a standard system of religious worship". [65] Further, King Ismail relied on use of force in order to promote Shiite sect, history has recorded that he used force at city of Tabriz, and justified his action by having a vision and in his vision Imam Ali told him; "let Qizilbash {in Azeri language means red head due to red hat they were wearing} be present in the mosque fully armed, encircling the worshippers; if anyone makes a move when the *khutba* (formal address in a mosque) is recited, the Qizilbash will be able to contain the situation".[66]

During Safavid dynasty, the Mullahs noticed that they were hot commodity and there was a high demand for them to promote Twelve Imam Shiite sect in Iran. The Safavid Kings gave permission to the Mullahs to be admitted to the king's palace and the Mullahs were able to gain ground in the King's palace and asking for privilege, "Shah Tahmasb showed great reverence to *sayyids* and bestowed on them honors and privileges, including land allotments".[67] These Mullahs were, "*Sayyids* are distinguished by their descent from Hashim, the house of the Prophet through patrilineal or matrilineal lines".[68] Once, the Mullahs established themselves in the King's palace the Mullahs, "openly declared that temporal authority belonged not to the Shah but to the *mujtahid* {prove of God on earth, which is another blasphemy, does God really need prove on earth?} of the time until the return of the Mahdi". [69] {Actually Koran has mentioned Jesus will come back to this world in order to save the world, and Koran does not mention anything about a person name Mehdi. Plus, Eleventh Imam did not marry to anyone, did not have concubine and would be impossible to have a child}.

The Mullahs wanted to become the King of Iran. On the other hand, public would not embrace the Mullahs as their authority because the Mullahs were factors of public out cry and it was recorded in Iran's history that "the *mohtaseb* is a thief and the *qadi* a bribe taker, The *sheikh al- eslam* is devil, the *mullah* a miserable wretch, In hell they make *boghra* soup which is waiting for the *sheikh* and the *mullah*".[70] "Keep a wary eye in front of you for a woman, behind you for a mule and from every direction for a *mulla*".[71]

King of Kings Ismail and his son Tahmasib invented Shiite sect to unify Iranian citizens against Ottoman Empire. The Kings utilized Mullahs as a fashion to unify Iranian citizens; the Mullahs would manipulate public feelings and exaggerated religious occurrences and would re-invent the religious occurrences in order Iranian citizens to become conscience with regard to political culture of just as well as to earn money. Mullah Kashef Sabzevar founder of Imam Hussein martyrdom, who exaggerated Imam Hussein's saga, Mullah Sabzevar was first person who introduced Imam Hussein Karbala saga and galvanized the Imam Hussein Karbala saga in Iranian culture. Mullah Sabzevar described the Karbala saga in a heartbreaking situation and other Mullahs learned from Mullah Sabzevar how to describe the Karbala saga in a mosque during sermon to people that how Imam Hussein revolted against the central government due to unjust rulers of his time particularly Yzed {Actually, Imam Hussein revolted against the central government because he believed because he was grandson of Prophet Muhammad he was the rightful person to rule and other rulers were unjust}. According to the Mullahs, Imam Hussein knew well that he would become a martyr but regardless of consequences he went to battlefield to face Yzed the unjust ruler.

The Mullahs would tell Imam Hussein story similar to this story. Imam Hussein with his family and seventy two comrades did not have water in the desert of Karbala, and when Hussein's half-brother Abulfaz went to well to bring water for them, Abulfaz was killed in a brutal manner. The Abulfaz story went as this that Abulfaz was carrying bags of water with two hands, godless enemy approached him and cut off one hand, and Abulfaz remained determine to carry all bags of water with other hand, enemy cut off his other hand, {now crowds in the mosque are crying and calling Hussein's name} now Abulfaz was carrying bags of water with his mouth, Abulfaz called to his family and said; "do not worry I am coming", a reader shall ask how Abulfaz could call for his family while he had bags of water in his mouth? Glad to ask this good question, please next time ask a Shiite Mullah and a Mullah will justify their lies to you. Kindly be advise to wear one pair of running shoes because you will be running for your life, {all of a sudden crowds became emotional and cried out loud, and shouting Hussein, Hussein and smacking themselves on chest, and shouting louder Hussein, Hussein and interesting part would be the time when a person pull a dagger and gave himself a small slit on top of his own head and everywhere became pool of blood, which is against Islam one to hurt his/her own body, but Mullahs love it, the more smacking, and more blood, the Mullahs possess more power of manipulation on naïve and simple minded people}. Abulfaz was carrying bags of water with his mouth and enemy killed him right on spot in front of thirsty children and women {mosque is full of crowds and everyone is crying} and Mullah went on and continued his Karbala saga how Hussein was beheaded by godless Shimr. {Some may think that I am joking, or pulling someone's leg, but what I am writing it is exactly what the Mullahs are telling Iranian people for past several centuries, and I have no reason to dislike any faith nor any religious sect group. I do not disrespect the Karbala event whatsoever} Sabzevar and other Mullahs would go in great details how unjustly Hussein became a martyr; the grandson of Prophet Muhammad peace upon him became martyr, true it was a sad story. However, the Mullahs were making money by telling fabricated stories and manipulating Iranian people's sentimental affectation toward Imam Ali and his son Imam Hussein. Iranian liked Imam Ali because when Arab conquered Iran, King of Kings Yezgerd Third escaped to safety and when Umor captured Iran. Umor had all he wanted he had booty and plenty of fresh meats for him and among these fresh meats there was a Persian Princess with name of Shahbanu, who was daughter of the King, and now she was in hand of enemy. Umor and his outlaw bandit wanted to sell Princess Shahbanu. But Imam Ali rejected the idea of selling the Persian Princess in a slave market because Ali had an alterative motive. Ali wanted Shahbanu for himself. Shahbanu out smart Ali {Ali was not a savvy person, he relied on his sword in order to cross his point} and Shahbnu did not marry Ali because the Persian Princess was Zoroastrian and this faith was promoting monogamy. The Persian Princess claimed that she did not want to offend Fatmeh daughter of Prophet Muhammad {Ali and Muhammad were blood related and were cousin} and wife of Imam Ali. Instead the Persian Princess got married with Imam Hussein, son of Imam Ali. Therefore, Iranian began to develop some kind of amicable attachment to Hussein because the Persian Princess was not sold in the slave market and the marriage between the Persian Princess and Hussein became a symbol of union and alliance between Hussein and Iranian.

Coming back to Karbala saga the Persian Princess was at the battle of Karbala with her husband Hussein and when she witnessed her husband was beheaded. She rode her horse and fled the battle scene. Enemy pursued her and according to the Mullah and Mullah's superstition the Persian Princess asked the mountain to open and guarded her. The mountain did open itself and closed and the mountain never re-opened. In reality, Arabs captured the Persian Princess and did what they were good at it.

The Karbala saga was not finished by death of Hussein, there was one part of the battle of the Karbala that the Mullahs omitted to tell Iranian that how one Iranian with name of Mokhtar seek justice after

Karbala battle for the Persian Princess death {apparently Iranians are good to do coup} Mokhtar ambushed his enemy at nigh and killed as many people as he could. Iranian people need to learn a lesson from Mokhtar that he did not lament, but he was a courageous person and defended the Persian Princess death. What Mokhtar did was according to his own time, now times have change and seeking justice by means of sword is unacceptable and unjustifiable. Quiet frankly, no one here is insinuating or promoting violence act in order to solve today's Iran political dilemma. Today's movement to save Iran from yoke of Mullahs dictatorship has to be peaceful as Dr. Babayan mentioned; "Ahura Mazda challenges the human being, whether king, priest, warrior, or herdsman, to attain the divine glory (*farr*), as angles and demons aid or obstruct mankind in this endeavor. At the apocalyptic conclusion of the war against untruth, the savior Saoyoshant-rising from the depths of Lake Frazdan, where the seed of Zarathustra is said to have been preserved will usher in the final triumph over evil. Good thoughts, good deeds, and good words are the weapons with which individuals will have to fight". [72]

The notion of just ruler has a significant meaning for Iranian people; the notion of a just ruler was incorporated in Iran's literature as well as Dr. Babayan mentioned; "It is Kaveh who reminds the prince Feraydun of the monarch's role in Iranian tradition:" Your duty as king is to let me have justice". [73] Naturally, a prince or a king has responsibility as well as accountability to give justice to his/her citizens. It is an insufficient to be a just ruler. Those who did wrong, the wrongdoer had to be brought to justice and to face their victims. Interrelating, one contemporary political issues that a prince or princess has to deliver just to His/Her citizens and with respect to this character with name of Akbar GANJI who was a hooligan during 2538 revolution. Additionally, Akbar GANJI was an executioner and worked for the Mullahs intelligent bureau. There are valid questions. How many people did he murder? How many Iranian ladies did he rape? And many more questions. Then, during students Reform Movement GANJI claimed that he rejected Khomeini kingdom with intention to deceive and to be embrace by his victims as a hero. Crown Prince Reza PAHLAVI Heir to Throne of Iran, Iranian citizens want justice from you and GANJI must be brought before International Tribunal to clear his name of any wrong doing or to face punishment of his crimes. There is a Persian expression that a person born wolf, always will be a wolf. GANJI is a wolf and always will be a wolf.

The Safavid dynasty was not anything similar to the Islamic Republic of Mullahs. The Safavid dynasty economically was well established, and citizens were enjoying economical advancement. In the seventeen century, Iranian citizens would sell silk in Europe in exchange for silver,[74] further to the note "the Persian interlude' also continued over Sulayman's reign: Iranian ceramics remained in great demand abroad, even after China resumed porcelain exports,"[75] and the Safavid dynasty national treasure was used for public charity needs. The national treasure was not meant for Kings' pleasure or to accumulated wealth for the Kings. Moreover, the Safavid Kings were unlike the Mullahs to legislated discriminatory laws toward Iranian ladies. The Iranian ladies under sovereignty of the Safavid Kings were in position to become Queen of Iran and to rule Iran justly, and when there was a coup in the palace in order to secure kingdom for a certain crown prince, according to Babayan; "all females, whether descended from male or female blood, could rule-a phenomenon particular to the Safavis. In seventeenth-century practices, in fact, female members were blinded as well as males".[76]

The Mullahs admitted to palace from time of the Safavid dynasty which was a big mistake. The greedy and jealous Mullahs would become a disaster for King of Kings Mohammad Reza PAHLAVI, who had to deal with the Mullahs cordially, the King was a religious person who was up holding Shiite sect doctrine in Iran and the King had to be a just ruler to his citizens.

In 1963, the King implemented White Revolution in Iran, the White Revolution illustrated the King persona as a religious and a just ruler for Iranian citizens, the White Revolution initially had six points, "1) a land reform program 2) granting women the right to vote and to be elected, 3) the sale of state-owned industries to the public, and 4) profit-sharing measures for industrials workers"[77] "5) Literacy Corps and 6) the Health Corps"[78] these initial six policies were meant to modernize Iran. However, people owned land or owned means of production did not favor the White Revolution. The land reform policy liberated serfs from feudal lords. The point of land reform was to ended feudalism in Iran and embarked Iran toward well calculated and moderate capitalist system.

Iranian citizens were pampered by King of Kings Mohammad Reza PAHLAVI and the King did not allow Iranian citizens to experience shift of economic system from feudalism to capitalism like European nations. In Europe, peasants were told by their landlords that the peasants were free from any obligation toward land and landlords had no obligation toward peasants. The feudal lords instructed the peasants to evacuate their property forthwith and peasants had to move to a city and to find a job for themselves. The feudal lords transformed to owner of means of production. The peasants merely had one power which was their labor power that they had to give-up their labor power for a wage. The peasants were forced to work in factories eighteen hours a day and children were cleaning chimney with their body due small size of their body could fit in the chimney, children of peasants would slid in the chimney and clean inside of it.

The King shifted Iran's economy from feudalism to capitalism in a fashion of win-win situation. The King gave portion of the land to serfs and the serfs became land owners, and feudal lords had lands too but now feudal lords had to work for themselves and enjoy their own fruit of labor. The King established a just kingdom as all citizens were equal and they were earning their income by their own merit, there was no favoritism. According to Dr. Shapur BAKHTIAR the White Revolution had one technicality issue. The White Revolution was not approved by the parliament.[79] Dr. BAKHTIAR was right that the King had to pass a motion for His White Revolution policy in the parliament, and when the King's motion was legislated, the King would be in position to implement his White Revolution policy. When the King took unilateral decision on the White Revolution policy, He took responsibility as well as accountability toward the White Revolution policy. In case, the White Revolution would not have positive output, the King had to carry the negative output on His shoulders.

The King also up-hold Islamic doctrine when the King brought forward "Reform of Electoral Law"[80]because the King believed; "in the Islamic era the high principles of Islam not only showed respect and proper appreciation of women but gave them rights which have still not been granted to women in certain progressive countries of the West."[81]The King believed Iranian women were as equal as men and Iranian women were as patriot as men due to one particular incident and how Iranian women illustrated their love toward divine mother land of Iran; "the Persian women supplied the answer. Out from their walled courtyards and harems marched three hundred of that weak sex, with the flush of undying determination in their cheeks. They were clad in their plain black robes with the white nets of their veils dropped over their faces. Many held pistols {that is sexy now} under skirts...Straight to the Majlis they went, and, gathered there, demanded of the President that he admit them all. What the grave deputies of the Land of the Lion and the Sun may have thought of this strange visitation is not recorded. The President consented to receive a delegation of them. In his reception-hall they confronted him, and lest he and his colleagues should doubt their meaning...to kill their own husbands and sons, and leave behind their own dead bodies, if the deputies wavered in their duty to uphold the liberty and dignity of the Persian people and nation. "May we not exclaim: All honor to the veiled women of Persia".[82] These courageous Iranian ladies were defending Iranian interests and must have equal rights as men to vote and to be elected to office, and not to face any kind of discriminatory laws.

According to Machiavelli people "are quicker to criticize than to praise the deeds of others"[83] the Mullahs and businessmen were quick judgers when the White Revolution was implemented. The Mullahs and businessmen thought that they would lose their possession and they provoked students against the White Revolution. The King commended to suppress the revolt because the students were burning building, public transit, they turned into a savage beast. The King had responsibility as well as accountability to establish social order and safety and security for everyone with intention for common benefit. Iran needed to grow and to make progress. In 1963, the King ended feudalist economic system by implementing His White Revolution in Iran. Iran embarked on moderate, well calculated plan toward capitalist system. The King redistributed land among serf, and serf was transformed into a proud land owner of villager. The feudal lord own portion of the land. The King also gave away his own land. Some shall say the King was following MACHIAVELLI doctrine too; as Machiavelli said that a prince; "to seem merciful, faithful, humane, forthright, religious, and to be so; but his mind should be not to be so".[84] Those who say that the King pretend to be generous, those have forgotten that the King ran food programs from grade one to grade twelve. Plus, there were grant programs for university students and overseas students were entitled for student grants. The university students would eat meal at university in Iran for free and would break soft drink beverage bottles just for fun.

The King's White Revolution was not an element of surprise for Iranian citizens; the King was contemplating on ingredients of the White Revolution prior to 1963. The blue print of the White Revolution was planned to modernize Iran "by 1959 we had well over 8,000 Government primary schools, an eighteen-fold increase compared to 1922, and nearly 1,100 Government secondary school, an increase of some twenty-three-fold...in our Government primary schools well over a million pupils were enrolled, while some 225, 000 students were attending the Government secondary schools. The later included technical schools, agriculture schools, teachers' training schools, schools of art and music, and secretarial school. To teach these young people we employed about 45,000 teachers; significantly, about a third of them were women".[85] The King mentioned; "I {the King} should personally like to see still further advances in broadening the opportunities of our women, my aim being that our women should enjoy the same basic rights as men".[86] The Tudeh Party or communist party wanted to repay their gratitude to the King by murdering Him. The Tudeh Party was a legal party at earlier time in Iran and decided to engage in act of terrorism. The King wrote in his book Mission for my Country; "the third incident was when, in February 1949, I was attending the annual commemoration of the founding of the University of Teheran. In military uniform, I was just about to enter the Faculty of Law building, where the ceremony was to be held, when suddenly shots rang out, and bullets came in my direction. Fanatics though it may seem, three of them passed through my military cap without touching my head. But the gunman's fourth shot penetrated my right cheekbone and came out under my nose. My would-be assassin-who had been posing as a photographer-was within six feet of me. He was now aiming his revolver at my heart. Both he and I sufficiently apart from the crowd for me to know he had a good clear field of fire. At such point-blank range, how could he miss? I can still remember my reactions at that instant. I thought, 'What should I do? Shall I jump on him? But if I approach him, I shall become a better target. Shall I run away? Then I shall be perfect target to be shot in the back. So I suddenly started shadow-dancing or feinting. He fired again, wounding me in the shoulder. His last shot struck in the gun. I had the queer and not unpleasant sensation of knowing that I was still alive. The man then threw down his gun and tried to escape, and in their fury at this assassination attempt, some of my young officers unfortunately killed him. He must have been a curious character. We discovered that he had been friendly with various arch-conservative religious fanatics, yet in his flat we found literature of the Tudeh or Communist Party". [87]

The King did not want to eradicate Tudeh Party from Iran, he wanted Tudeh Party to flourish in Iran, and people to enjoy divers political life, he knew that "not only did army retain a significant number of Tudeh Party sympathizers and radicals who looked with interest at events in Egypt". [88] The King was confident that He could reign in Iran, and was not worry about Tudeh Party to infiltrate in Iran's army.

The left wing groups enhanced their terrorist activities in Iran, "in February 1971, thirteen young men attacked a Gendermarie post in the village of Siakal, killing three Gendarmes. They fled into the forests but were captured and executed". [89] No one forced the terrorist to open fire at a Gendermarie and once SAVAK would knock these terrorist doors, all of a sudden International Organizations would transform a terrorist person to a political activist, and SAVAK as a protector of citizens would become the bad guy. The International Organizations played dirty politics with Iranian citizens. The International Organizations protected terrorist individuals from judicial system and wanted terrorist individuals to be free and did what they wanted in Iran.

The King became sovereign of Iran the time when it was; "mid 1941 during Allied occupation of Iran. At that time, the country population was around 14 million, 78 percent of which lived in rural areas. Feudal land ownership prevailed in the country, the illiteracy rate was over 80 percent". [90] The King inherit a country that in 1941 over eighty percent of population was illiterate and by1979 fifty percent of population was illiterate. The number of illiterate people was on decline.

The King was given land deeds to a serf. Now she owns a land and no longer was a servitude to a feudal lord. God Bless Our King PAHLAVI.

The King's Land Reform Policy was people's will, and King did not imposed his land reform, "Persia is making striking progress, politically, economically, and socially. My people refuse to tolerate any longer a situation in which a few great land barons control the lives and destinies of thousands of peasants, many of whom live in utter poverty. So, in addition to distributing the Crown and Government holdings, we are going to divide up the large private estates".[91]

The King distributed oil revenue with Iranian citizens and there was a question, "who are the owners of the vast array of facilities that go to make up our oil industry? *The people of Iran own them all.* from this circumstance my countrymen and I drive much satisfaction; it gratifies our national pride to know that our entire oil industry belongs to us alone".[92] According to Ganji, "the GNP increased more than thirteen times, from little over $4 billion in 1962 to over $53 in 1976. per capita income went up eight times from $195 to $1,600 in the same period and increased further to $2,400 in 1978". [93] According to the King; "in response to my call the minister of OPEC met in Teheran on December 22 and 23, 1973. This assembly decided to raise the price of each barrel of oil from 5.032 to 11.651 dollars. Earlier that year during Arab oil embargo, we had sold oil on the spot market for $35 a barrel".[94] In 1979, Iran sold one barrel of oil for $40.00 U.S which was according to equilibrium price.

In 2006, the price of oil is sky rocket, and when the King mentioned in His book Answer to History that the biggest loser in this revolution will be the American. Indeed, the Americans are buying one barrel of oil for over $70.00 U.S. and have to deal with nuclear bombs of the Mullahs and the Mullahs are supporting global terrorism.

Iran was making progress and the King was responding to His citizens' needs and wants. However, the left wing groups and fanatic Muslims were not satisfied with the Kings hard work and accusing him of stealing money from treasury. The left wing groups and the Mullahs would point their finger to homeless and working ladies in field of oldest profession in street as a reason that the King was stealing money from treasury. The left wing groups and Khomeini besmirched the King because the left wing groups and Khomeini, "and first among the means which a citizen has used to become great is to accuse falsely. When used against powerful citizens who are opposed to his desire for power, such means are very effective, for through them he can take side of the people and can make them his friend by confirming their low opinion of his opponents".[95]

In 2565/2006 the Mullahs are stealing from Iran's treasury. Simply, comparing today's life with respect to 2538/1979 the King's time, "before the revolution, the toman [Iran's currency] was strong. It was seven tomans to the dollar: Now it is eight hundred," he said, then paused again and repeated the figured:"eight hundred".[96] Iranian citizens during reign of the King could buy one U.S. dollar for seven tomans. Now, Iranian subjects have to pay eight hundred tomans. Further, at the time of the King Iranian citizens would show their passport to any embassy and they were welcome to a county. Now, if anyone shows up with the Mullah passport, the host country is reluctant to issue a visa.

The left wing groups and the Mullahs armed themselves with strong words and accusation that the King was wasting Iranian oil revenue by purchasing arsenal. The left wing groups and the Mullahs had forgotten those days when Britain and Russia were invading pure mother land of Iran at their will. The left wing groups and the Mullahs intentionally were deceiving Iranian citizens by their besmirch and were holding back knowledge that Iran's geo-politically was located in political realism, "human nature is evil, the desire for power is instinctive to all individuals and cannot be eliminated, international politics is a struggle for power, in such a environment states must ultimately rely on their own efforts to ensure their own security, military power and preparedness is the most important factor in determining state power and security and economic issues are less relevant to national security".[97] The King was dictated by his neighboring countries in order to enhance its military force with intention to create peace in Iran and stability in the Middle East. The King's expenditure on Iran's army "by this calculation the money spent on our arm forces is about 17% of the country's budget, and comparing this sum with 50% of Switzerland, the 75% of Pakistan, or the nearly 50% of India it is very little".[98] In 1977, the King increased defence expenditure "more than 35 percent of the budget was associated with defence expenditure, and 35 percent went to development expenditure".[99] The King had to invest in Iran's army in order to deter Russia and Iraq to invade Iran. If the King did not modernize Iran's army as Machiavelli mentioned that the King had to rely on his Fortune not to be invaded by other countries, and other countries would invade a weak country, which was the case in 1991 when Iraq invaded Kuwait.

From north Russia wanted to fulfill its long dream of Peter the Great to capture Persian Gulf. From West Saddam Hussein wanted to take Khozestian province for oil reason. In 1974, former permanent President of Iraq SADDAM disputed the King's naming of a river Alvand Rood which was between Iran and Iraq. The King commended to His army to deploy and to launch an assault on Iraq territory. SADDAM realized that the King was not a pussy cat, He was a Persian Lion and was about to bite Iraq once for all. SADDAM apologized to the King and the river was called Alvand Rood. When the King decided not to attack to Iraq two sergeants committed suicide because they were disappointed when they heard the King's command of not attacking to Iraq.

In 1978, the King was preoccupied in Iran with internal conflicts, there was an opportunity for Russia to invade Afghanistan and when in 1980 the King passed away Iraq invaded Iran. The region of Middle East fully defined the term political realism.

In 1980, SADDAM decided to wage war against Iran over Alvand Rood River. The big Persian Lion was not around to roar at a mouse SADDAM {American soldiers pulled SADDAM out of a hole, he was a mouse} SADDAM wanted to become the leader Arab nations and he glamorized the Battle of Qaddsieh. SADDAM called himself commander of the Battle of Qaddsieh.

Khomeini did not call himself Rustam, there was another story for Khomeini to have invaders in divine land of Iran. According to Khomeini war was good for clerics' business because the Mullahs would attend a funeral for dead soldiers and would make earning. Furthermore, the Iran and Iraq war was a gift for the Mullahs because the Mullah could secure their theology kingdom. The Iranian people would go to battlefield and died, and there was no opposition voice. The Iranian people were preoccupied to defend their country against Iraqi aggressor. The Mullahs took full advantage of the war which was used as a tool to fight with Iranian culture. Iranian celebrates first day of spring which is about March 20th {spring equinox} and called New Year *Nou Roz*. {Also, not only Mullahs hate *Nou Roz* Osama Bin Laden hated *Nou Roz* too and was not allowing Afghan people to celebrate *Nou Roz*} at the time of the war the Mullahs deployed massive number of soldiers to battlefield and would use wave of human to clear landmines in order to reclaim Iranian territory. Consequently, massive number of soldiers lost their life to reclaim Iran's territory. When the New Year would come Iranian people did not celebrate New Year, Iranian people were mourning for their love one that they were perished in the war zone. Iranian people were mourning rather than celebrating and enjoying life, and that was what Khomeini promised to Iranian citizens that everyone would become happy under his kingdom.

All in all, the King was an absolute ruler who brought prosperity and peace for Iranian citizens and region. The King implemented the White Revolution policy which was corner stone of His absolute rule in Iran and Iran flourished at rapid pace, He modernized Iran's economic system, the feudal system was scrapped and replaced by the modern capitalist system, as well as, the King modernized Iran's army as a mean to deter foreign nations to invade Iran. Most importantly, Iranian ladies were on His top priority to be as equal as men. On the other hand, Khomeini brought misery and disaster for proud Iranian citizens, particularly Iranian ladies became non class citizens, not even second class citizen because second class citizen has rights, in case of non class citizen has absolutely no rights.

"The Islamic Republic of Mullah in Iran Is a Dictator State"

O n February 01ˢᵗ, 1979 Khomeini HENDI arrived at Mehr Abad Airport at city of Tehran. He was ushered with several air force technicians known as *Homafar*, the *Homafar* rank in Iran's military was not a sergeant and was not an officer, the *Homafar* rank was allocated in the Military Air Force strictly. The *Homafars* ushered Khomeini to a cemetery south of city of Tehran with name of Beheshteh Zahra {Behesht means paradise, and paradise was an actual Persian word which integrated to Greek language and from Greek language was transmitted to English language. During ancient Iran, Iranians were known to enjoy gardening, and planting. The Iranian kings would take part with their fellow citizens and would do gardening and planting, and Iranian kings called garden paradise}. Khomeini gave a speech and in his speech he said that Lion and Sun had to be removed from Iran's flag, as well all court documents, and everywhere which had Lion and Sun symbols must be removed at once because Lion and Sun were signs of rebellion. He referred to symbols of Lion and Sun with an Arabic word "*Taghoot*". The Mullahs were using Arabic words because Iranian people speak Persian language and Iranian people would not understand what the Mullahs were saying, the message became ambiguous for ordinary person and an ordinary person might think that the Mullahs were intellectuals.

Coming to this point that Khomeini called the Lion and Sun symbols were indications of rebellion. Actually, Khomeini was absolutely correct that the Lion and Sun were symbols of rebellion. The Lion was symbol of bravery {*Zhe-an*} courage, and fearless and Sun was associated with religion of Zoroastrian, the faith of Zoroastrian had Iranian root which promoted unity of one God, and established on three premises, Good Thoughts, Good Deeds, and Good Words and unlike Islam which was an alienated faith to Iranian, and every Mullah called himself sign of god and theologically Mullahs and their hooligans could lie and was not a sin. As Dr. Babyan quoted from Ferdowsi poem; "caravan dog [*karivani*] cannot bring down a roaming lion. The reference to the Arab Bedouins as caravan dog is clear, but is Ferdowsi voicing sedition through his ideal king Kay Khusraw? Are Iranian youth being reminded that they are lions not to be defeated by Arabs {Bedouins}?"[100] The symbol of Lion on Iran's flag was symbol of bravery of Iranian people and to remind Iranian people to take stand against Arab Bedouins invaders. Khomeini *Sayyed* which means in Arabic language "Mr." in Iran *"Sayyed"* is associated with people who are descendant of Prophet Muhammad Arab Bedouins Tribe. Khomeini from Arab Bedouins Tribe hated Iran and Iranian people, and hated everything Iran stood for. Khomeini was the hungry dog and hated Iranian symbol of Lion which was a reminder to Iranian to defend their nation against Arab Bedouins like Khomeini. Therefore, Khomeini HENDI Arab Bedouins removed the Lion from Iran's flag as a reason that he defeated proud and brave Iranian people.

This dog caravan of Arab Bedouins Tribe invader of Iran, which was land of lion and sun needed to understand that the Lion symbol was incorporated in Iran's culture, and the Lion was not just on Iran's flag, the Lion face could be seen on Iranian sword that the sword had two lion faces at the beginning of the handle, and word sword in Persian language is written and pronounced *"shamshir"*. The Lion in Persian language is written and pronounced *"shir"*. Is there a coincident that word sword and word lion sharing one word of lion? Furthermore, the beauty of lion was used at the time when ancient Iranian citizens would drink water in Persian Rhyton Lion cup.

This dog caravan of Arab Bedouins Tribe invaders of divine mother land of Iran did not stop their hostility on Iran's national flag. In 1980, the Mullahs abandoned Iran's Red Lion and Sun Society because the Society had Lion and Sun as an emblem. The Mullahs worked hard to disband the Red Lion and Sun Society; the Mullahs were defeated in their plan to disband the Red Lion and Sun emblem at the Geneva Conventions which has recognized since 1949 the Red Lion and Sun emblem as humanitarian services. According to Dr. Bahman Aghi Diba {International Law} "the authorities of the Islamic Republic of Iran {Mullah, Iran is a great name and cannot be associated with the dog caravan of Arab Bedouins Tribe} tried at least for several years and spent a considerable amount of money and energy, especially through the Iranian Ministry of Foreign Affairs, to eradicate the emblem and join the Red Crescent. This was one of the ugliest acts of regime for eradicating a purely Iranian sign that had nothing to do with the Pahalvi dynasty {In 1922, International Committee of the Red Cross accepted Iranian Red Lion and Sun Society and In 1927, Iranian Red Lion and Sun Society joined International Federation of Red Cross Societies} or the monarchial system in Iran. The hostility of the Islamic regime with the Red Lion and Sun was on only a kind of blind enmity towards everything Iranian and different than the Arab invaders of Iran...The sign of the Red Lion and Sun has been a symbol of Iran for centuries and for those who are interested in religion stories, it has even religious and Shiite justifications {because Imam [Imam means in Arabic language a leader] Ali who was first Shiite sect leader, he was associated with lion}...The Iranian "diplomats" succeed to pay for the expenses of having such a conference and they made contacts with many countries (offering them various incentives) to help convene a conference to amend the statues of the Movement and omit the Iranian sign. However, happily the "representatives of Iran" failed to eradicate this Iranian sign from the list of the emblem of the ICRC...the Red Crescent (originally an Islamic Sunni sign of the concerned organizations)".[101]

This dog caravan of Arab Bedouins Tribe invader of Iran and their leader Khomeini had hostility toward Iran's culture and Iranian identity and did not have an intention to build Iran but to destroy Iran and the Iranian culture as well as Iranian identity. A prudent person would come to this natural conclusion that Khomeini hated Iran period and everything stand in the name of Iran or anything symbolized Iran and identified Iran as a distinct nation compare to its neighboring nations.

On April 01st, 1980 or April fools day Khomeini established his own Islamic Republic of Mullah in Iran and took Iranians as a hostage. Khomeini proceeded by approving one type of political party which was called Party of God "Hezbollah Party". There was an inherit problem to have one type of political party in one country. Especially, Iran was a diverse country ideologically as well as ethnicity. Once, there was one political party, and there was not allow another political party to participate during election time. The one political party system was absorbed in the state ideology and the one political party system was representing interest of the state and not diversity of citizens from ideologically and ethnicity aspects.

This dog caravan of Arab Bedouins Tribe, their leader Khomeini HENDI established his theology kingdom when Khomeini commenced to murder the Kings' army personnel in cold blood. Once, Khomeini was finished with murdering the King army personnel, Khomeini and his hooligans continue assaulting, insulting and deformation of character to the King's army personnel at every given occasions that the King's army personnel were having better quality of life than others. Khomeini HENDI and hooligans abused and besmirched has been continuing and thinking that they could have done better, and fact of reality proved that they are incompetent people.

Once, Khomeini became sure that the King's army was no threat to his new found dog caravan of Arab Bedouins kingdom in Iran, Khomeini opened another butcher shop to eliminate political competition and to secure his kingdom, this butcher shop was dedicated for left wing groups, and the left wing groups were mob enforcers of Khomeini, the left wing groups delivered and presented Khomeini to political kingdom of Persia. Khomeini was horny for power of politics he would do anything to secure his kingdom and did not want to share his new found political power with anyone. Khomeini commenced to sharp his knives like a good butcher who sharps his knives before the butcher slaughters his animals, and Khomeini had sharp knives and commenced to murder and raped as many as the left wing groups as he could with assistance of his hooligans in order to create a fearful state. Khomeini failed to understand that murdering new found subjects was not key factor for him to remain in power because when Khomeini and hooligans were murdering their new found subjects, they were creating hate atmosphere, and according to MACHIAVELLI whenever there was a hate atmosphere the state had no public support and the state remained fragile and vulnerable to eternal force and could collapse at any time. Public wanted to improve their well being and put stop in bloodshed. Thus, public would join external force to oust the instigators in Iran.

Khomeini was busying with murdering Iranians and the other Mullahs were busy stealing money from Iranians. This accusation that the Mullahs were robbing Iranian people was not a deformation of character to this dog caravan of Arab Bedouins. According to Forbes issued an article with title of "Millionaire Mullahs" by Paul KLEBNIKOV who mentioned "a nuclear threat to the rest of the World, Iran is robbing its own people of prosperity. But the men at the top are getting extremely rich"[102] KLEBNIKOV stated that when students were gathered in street and expressing their dissatisfaction to the Mullahs; "a gang of 30 motorcycle, brandishing iron bars and clubs as big as baseball bats, roars through the stalled traffic. They glared at the drivers, yell threats, thump cars, burly and bearded, {there are pictures which regards to other events which occurred that a reader will see before their own two eyes, how Iranian people are getting beat up by this Arab Bedouins} the bikers yank two men from their auto and pummel them... the Islamic Republic is a strange dictatorship. As it moves to repress growing opposition to clerical rule, the regime relies not on soldiers or uniform police, {if the state relies on the army, there will be coup, the Mullahs know better} but on the bullies of Hezbollah and the equally thuggish Revolutionary Guards. The powers that be claimed to derive legitimacy from Allah".[103] The Mullahs in Iran used force as a means in order to suppress opposition voice and using religion as a tool in order to justify their dictatorship. When the Mullahs are calling themselves Ayatollahs which means sign of God, the Mullahs actually mean that they do not have to answer to anyone except God and relinquished responsibility and accountability toward their citizens and citizens are transformed to a servitude subject. The top dog among Mullah is Ali Akbar Hashemi Rafsanjani "..."father of Iran's privatization" program. During his presidency the stock market was opened up to private companies. Most of the good properties and contracts, say dissident member of Iran's Chamber of Commerce, ended up in the hands of mullahs, their associates and, not least, Rafsanjani's own family, who rose from modest origins as small-scale pistachio farmers...Rafsanjani's sons took key position in the Ministry of Oil; another son heads the Tehran Metro construction project".[104] There was a problem for Iranian people that Mullah Rafsanjani's sons were posted to a position that they did not have proper qualifications nor merit for their posts. Rafsanjani's sons took the post due to their father's influence in the Mullah kingdom. Rafsanjani was not a petty thief, Rafsanjani one of children of Prophet Muhammad was "stashing billion of dollars in bank accounts in Switzerland and Luxembourg; controlling huge swaths of waterfront in Iran's free economic zones on the Persian Gulf...beaches of Dubai, and Goa Thailand...Rafsanjani's youngest son, Yaser, owns a 30-acres horse farm in the super-fashionable Lavasan neighborhood of north Tehran, where land goes for over $4 million an acre. Just where did Yaser get his money? A Belgian-educated businessman, he runs a large export-import firm that includes baby food, bottled water and industry machinery".[105] When Iranian people will liberate Iran from yoke of Mullahs, Iranian people will slam civil actions on the Rafsanjani and other Mullahs doors plus the hooligans doors, the stolen money will be return to rightful owners plus interests.

Iranian people has been aware of the Rafsanjani and other Mullahs grand theft of Iran's wealth "typical *Agha-zadehs* {translating Agha-zadeh. Agha means Mr., Zadeh means born, translating in English language to best of my knowledge, it means born with silver spoon in his mouth} are Mehdi and Yasser Rafsanjani, sons of the ex-president. A journalist (who was later imprisoned) once asked ex-president Rafsanjani: How has your son become one of the richest men in Iran? Rafsanjani's impassive response was: 'Why don't you go and ask him?'"[106] , and when the reporter asked where did Rafsanjani's sons brought the hard core cash to buy mansions and luxury, the reporter was incarcerated.

Clearly, Mullah Rafsanjani and many other Mullahs are stealing from Iranian people and when a small own of a store is making a few penny, the local Mullah "will come to you and ask for a contribution to his local charity," says an opposition economist, who declines to give his name. "If you refuse, you will be accused of not being a good Muslim. Some witnesses will turn up easily that they heard you insult the Prophet Mohammad, and you will be thrown in jail".[107] The Mullahs had been hungry dogs, and never could be satisfied the poor dogs were looking for food always and would use deceptive means to satisfy their hungry feelings. On the other hand, the Iranian people were not pussy cat and bow down to Arab Bedouins; the Iranian people are defying Mullahs at every given opportunity; "no wonder so many students turn to the streets in protest. The dictatorship tells them what to think, what to wear, and what to eat and drink. It has also been robbing them of their future".[108] On Friday July 09th, 2004 Mr. KLEBNIKOV was assassinated in Moscow. Kindly, do not be surprise that Mr. KLEBNIKOV was murdered, the Mullahs will murder anyone in name of Almighty Allah, and after murdering someone, the murderers will shout God is Great.

When Rafsanjani and other Mullahs are children of Prophet Muhammad plus hooligans has been taking away without color of rights from Iranian people and Iranian people are victims of the Mullahs and the hooligans thievery it has adverse effect on Iranian people;" Khomeini swept to power with promise of independence, freedom and an Islamic classless society. Today, according to the regime's own figure, 15 per cent of the population lives blew poverty line and the unemployment rate among people under 30 is about 28.4 per cent. Writing in Le Figaro in February 2001, the historian Houshang Nahavandi noted that Iran's per capita income in 1977 was $2,450 and by all accounts this would be comparable in the year 2000 to $10,000, close to that of Spain. It is, at present, less than $1,500, near to that of…the Gaza Strip"[109].

On January 16th, 1979 the King of Kings Mohammad Reza PAHLAVI First left Iran and relinquished responsibility, as well as, accountability of Iran in hands of a regency government of Dr. Shapour BAKHTIAR, who was a socialist. Dr. BAKHTIAR was a well known political character in Iran's political stage and he did not get a long very well with the King. Dr. BAKHTIAR did not hate or resent the King. Dr. BAKHTIAR had legitimate issues with the King over certain policies; such as, the White Revolution policy, the King did not draft the White Revolution policy in parliament, the King took unilateral approach toward the White Revolution policy.

Dr. BAKHTIAR was not on side of the Mullahs. Dr. BAKHTIAR was well educated from France; he earned his PhD in field of political science at Sorbonne, Paris and enlisted in French army during World War Two. When Dr. BAKHTIAR became a regency government of Iran, the Iranians identify him as a socialist and not communist. Dr. BAKHTIAR asked Iranian to remain calm and asked for three months to improve Iran's economy. He was loved by people, Iranians stopped their demonstrations and situation was contained. The former Democrat president of the U.S. Jimmy CARTER and his Administration stated that they supported Dr. BAKHTIAR. The Iranians got emotional that Dr. BAKHTIAR was a puppet of the U.S. and Iranians came out of their home and took streets one more time. Dr. BAKHTIAR could not manage the regency government and his regency government collapsed less than two months. Dr. BAKHTIAR was forced to go on exile and he resided in France. When he was in France, he was broadcasting to Iran via and he encouraged Iranians to engage in non-violence movement in Iran. Dr. BAKHTIAR was a solid political figure and everyone would listen to him.

On July 1980, Dr. BAKHTIAR escaped assassination attempt and this assassination cost two individual's life. One French police officer and one neighbor were dead. On August 07th, 1991 Dr. BAKHTIAR was murdered along with his secretary Soroush KATIBEH at his home.

Switzerland police apprehended one culprit in his role to murdered Dr. BAKHTIAR, the culprit was an element of the Islamic Republic of Mullah, and extradited the culprit to France for prosecution. In 1994, the accused person during course criminal trial revealed that French Secret Police was involved in assassination of Dr. BAKHTAIR.

The Democrat U.S. Administration and Jimmy CARTER were deeply involved in ousting the King from His Throne and assisted Khomeini in power in Iran. The Democrat Administration was involved in murdering one of the King's men with name of Ali Akbar Tabatabai who was the King's former press attaché. In 1980, the Mullah recruited one African-American with name of David Belfield, he converted to Islam and changed his name to Hassan Abdulrahman at city of Washington, D.C. the Democrat Administration took part in assassinating Mr. Tabatabai by allowing Abdulrahman to wear U.S. postal uniform and knocked Mr. Tabatabai door. When Mr. Tabatabai answered the door and opened the door, Abdulrahman was holding a parcel with his hand and appeared to Tabatabai that Abdulrahman was a postal worker and Abdularahman called Mr. Tabatabi name. Mr. Tabatabai acknowledged to Abdulrahman that he was Tabatabi. Then, Abdulrahman opened fired at Tabatabai with a pistol and murdered Tabatabai. Abdulrahman escaped scene of crime and entered on Canadian soil and had pre-arranged air plane ticket at Province of Québec. He flew from Canada to Iran and took shelter in Iran. The U.S. justified their action to assist the Mullahs to murder Tabatabai because the Mullahs attacked at U.S. embassy and took American citizens hostage. Interestingly, when the hooligans like Asgharzadeh, and Mirdamad took the embassy and took hostages, the hooligans took some low rank soldiers and low statues diplomats. The hooligans did not take high ranking officers or diplomats as hostages.

There was one more circumstantial evidence that Jimmy CARTER Democrat Administration signed Algris Accord with the Mullahs. There was one negotiator behalf of Khomeini with name of Mehdi BAZARGAN signed the Algris Accord, and this Accord provided arsenal to the Mullahs and assurance from the U.S. not to intervene in Iran's domestic politics.

The Democrat Administration was running propaganda machine to their citizens that the U.S. was in confrontation with Iran and in reality the U.S. was not in confrontation with Iran. Moreover, the U.S.

was in proxy war with the former Soviet Union, and battle ground was Afghanistan. There was one incident which revealed that the U.S. was having a proxy war with former Soviet Union when one of U.S. arsenal shipment to the Afghan fighters against the former Soviet Union took wrong turn. The incident occurred when Red Army of the former Soviet Union became aware that the U.S. was supplying arsenal to Afghan fighters, the U.S. was utilizing Iran's air space and Iran's secret military air base. When the U.S. cargo planes were positioned at the secret air base by desert of Tabas, which was located by Afghanistan and Iran border and the airbase was not close by city of Tehran.

The former Soviet Union's Red Army located the cargos and fired rockets at the U.S. cargo planes and the U.S. cargo planes were engulf of flames and their mission was revealed to everyone that the U.S. was assisting the Afghan fighters while the U.S. was utilizing Iran's air space as well as land. Immediately the Democrat Administration claimed that there was a secret mission to save hostages from the Mullahs. The hostages were located in city of Tehran not by Afghanistan and Iran border.

The U.S. tobacco and alcohol bureau was busy selling arsenal to Iran. The U.S. was enjoying lucrative arsenal deal to the Mullahs. Eventually, Iran-Contra Scandal emerged which caused damaged on Republican Administration also Israel was making arsenal deal with the Mullahs on "August 18, 1982: U.S. intelligence reports indicated that Israel continues to ship arms to Iran. A recent deal between the two countries reportedly involved up to $50 million worth of material, possibly including arms Israel captured from the Palestine Liberation Organization in Lebanon. The Israel government acknowledges it has been selling spare aircraft parts including replacement to Iran".[110]

The U.S. and Israel were not only benefactor of the Mullah state. Yaser Arafat was deeply involved in Iran's revolution. In 2537/1978 Arafat dispatched his own hand picked terrorists, natural born Palestine killers, on Iran's soil at the time of revolution and these terrorists would join among mobs and concealed their weapons and would open fire directly at Iranian rebellious during revolt in order to cause chaos, and were murdering mobs and most importantly these Palestine natural born killers were murdering the King's soldiers. In addition, Arafat collaborated with the Mullahs to trained terrorists on Palestine soil.

Then, the Mullahs terrorist would come back to Iran and engaged in terrorist activities on Iran's soil. There was one well known terrorist character with name of Chamron who was trained on Palestine soil, and returned to Iran and engaged in terrorist activities.

In 1979, the Palestinian people in Iran under command of infamous terrorist Arafat, when the King's Army personnel were sentenced to capital punishment at Alavi School at city of Tehran. The natural born Palestine terrorists would take pride and glory to kill the King's Army personnel. As a matter of fact, Madam Afschineh Latifi in her book "Even After All This Time: A Story of Love, Revolution and Leaving Iran" stated that she observed two militant Palestinians in her house and there was one militant Palestinian was playing with a toilet flush and was amused with the toilet flush, and kept flushing the toilet, until her mother stopped the armed Palestinian from flushing the toilet.

King of Kings Mohammad Reza PAHLAVI in his book; *"Answer to History"* mentioned that the U.S. will be the biggest loser for assisting Khomeini to ousting the PAHLAVI dynasty. In 2006, world is buying one barrel of oil for over seventy dollars U.S. which is not according to equilibrium price. The price of oil is sky rocket because the Middle East region is in chaos. The Middle East became chaotic because former U.S. President CARTER made a poor judgment and a poor policy, he thought by ousting the King he would be able to reduce the price of oil and sell arsenal at high price. CARTER failed to make a prudent calculation that the Mullahs had their own agenda and one day the Mullahs would attack at U.S. soil and the U.S. interest globally at some point in future. Regrettably, the September 11th, 2001 was an avoidable matter. The King and his army personnel kept the Middle East in peace without bloodshed. For example, Saddam Hussein never would dare to launch an attack on Kurdish village {Halebcheh} and using chemical and biological arsenal on villagers and killing innocent people. The King was not using force; the King was a savvy and a prudent person, who was using his political skills. Once, former Prime Minister of Canada Lester B. Pearson said; "politics are the skilled use of blunt objects". King of Persia, King of Kings Mohammad Reza PAHLAVI was using his talent and skill to keep the Middle East in peace, and when the Middle East was in peace, the world was in peace. As long as the Mullahs are ruling in Iran, the world shall be insecure place to be. Particularly the Mullahs are having nuclear capability and the Mullahs will spread their domination globally.

The King had made several nuclear facilities in Iran and the project were intended to generate electricity for Iranian citizens and was not plan to built nuclear bomb. In 2537/1978 the Mullahs like Khameini, Rafsanjani, and Khatami with other Mullahs with their associate hooligans were spreading rumors that the King had diabolic plan, the King wanted to make Iranian men impotent. In 2006, Khameini, Rafsanjani, and Khatami and other Mullahs with their hooligan associates are claiming the nuclear capability is Iran's legal right and the Mullahs must have nuclear capability. The Mullahs are making parallel reasoning as Dr. Mohammad MUSSADIQ as He nationalized Iran's oil. However, Dr. MUSSADIQ never had a plan to committee genocide. Why do the Mullahs want to have nuclear capability? The King asked the same above question. What will the Mullahs do with the nuclear plants in Iran that the King built? [iii] Answering the question, there was a problem with a dictator state for rest of the world. The dictator state inherently had planed to expand their fanatic ideology globally. In case of the Islamic Republic of Mullah was not any different, the fanatic Muslim wanted to expand their ideology globally. Mullah Khameini hand picked a president for Iranian people, the selected President is Mahmoud Ahmedi Nezhad who was an executioner during revolution and a rapist, the selected President wants to have a nuclear bomb in order to wipe state of Israel and the President's priority agenda is to resurrect the Hidden Imam as soon as possible. There is a chilling story for anyone is dealing with the cold blooded murderers Mullahs to have a nuclear capability. According to fanatic Muslim the only time, the Hidden Imam will resurrect from hidden when the world is in total chaos, and the Hidden Imam will resurrect from hidden in order to enforce world Islamic orders. Karl MARX also gave a promise of utopian society and predicted collapse of capitalism. MARX assumed in his theory that in a capitalist system there is a social stratification and in this system of social stratification people are divided by three classes, one bourgeois, two petite bourgeois and last proletarian. Each class was divided according to their socioeconomic possession. Further, MARX believed petite bourgeois would absolved in the proletarian class because price of goods were increasing and there would be a handful of bourgeois class who had and big segment of a society did not have and this was mass proletarian class who would revolt and establish the utopian society. Nice fairy tail, there never will be a day to establish utopian society because there is limited of natural resources.

There were some politicians, who were naïve and simple mind, and they deemed they could flirt with Islamic Republic of Mullah and did not get hurt by the fanatic Muslim Mullahs. This type of politicians same as former President of the U.S.A CARTER were making poor judgment, these peculiar politicians were flirting {Las} with the Mullahs because there was an economical gain for them. Particularly, in Canada, the Liberal Party on federal level flirted with the Mullahs which became evident at the time of death of Madam Zahra KAZEMI.

On June 2003 Ms. Zahra KAZEMI Iranian-Canadian photo journalist died in hands of her interrogators at Evin prison. On March 31st, 2005 Dr. Shahram Azam, received political asylum from Canada because he was the doctor who examined Madam KAZEMI. Dr. AZAM noted that Ms. KAZEMI sustained "bruised from forehead to ear, skull fracture, two broken fingers, broken and missing fingernails, severe abdominal bruising, evidence of 'very brutal rape' swelling behind the head, burst ear membrane, bruised shoulder, deep scratches on the neck, broken 'nose-bone', evidence of flogging to the legs, and crushed big toe"[112] the Liberal Government did nothing to defend Madam KAZEMI's death. The Liberal Government continued their business as usual and let Human Right Abuse to pass by as if nothing occurred. According to Canadian Broadcasting Corporation {C.B.C} "Canada willing to help Iran, despite Kazemi row"[113] it was published Friday April 01st, 2005 "Iran had requested that one of its officials, Seyed Abu Talib Najafi, be briefed on the workings of Canada's new Advance Passenger Information database, designed to identify potential threats to civil aircraft before they board"[114] did the Liberal Government providing training facility for a the Mullah terrorist? Yes. Furthermore, "according to e-mails obtained under the Access to Information Act, Customs officials were concerned about the visit becoming public. One e-mail said: "We should keep this as low-key as possible"[115]. The Liberal Party as a Government of Canada had more than one incident such as above one. If anyone wanted to tab the Mullahs and the Liberal Government relation, it would be like opening a Pandora box. In addition, the C.B.C is very protective toward the Mullahs and if there is any kind of news with regard to the Mullahs and how Iranians were revolting to their current theology state and Iranians were disregarding the theology state and were regarding the theology state as an illegitimate state. The

C.B.C does not air any story with regard to the unstable theology state of the Mullah. The C.B.C news refrained to air any programs that how the Mullahs and hooligans were violating Human Rights in Iran and has been keeping Canadian and Iranian-Canada in absent mind as if everything was all well in Iran. Such as, this particular incident which captured whole European nations and the U.S. media outlet except the C.B.C, when one group of Iranians decided to create a safer world for everyone "BRUSSELS, Belgium (AP) – Police on Friday said they'd removed a group of 56 unarmed passengers of Iranian origin encamped on a Lufthansa jetliner who'd said they wouldn't leave until the United States and other nations signed a pledge not to help Iran's "Islamic regime of Mullahs".[116] The people who bored on plane and refused to leave the plane were trespassers, and could not achieve their goal, but this group proved that this group did not want the Mullahs to have access to nuclear capability.

There was a down fall for Canadian when the C.B.C was protecting the Mullahs by not reporting their Human Rights Violation to Canadian. In 2006, Conservative Party formed a government in Canada and Honorable Prime Minister of Canada Stephen HARPER has taken firm position against the Mullahs and terrorism. On June 02nd, 2006 news broke out that seventeen men were apprehended by the Canadian Security Intelligence Service {CSIS} and Royal Canadian Mount Police {R.C.M.P} because the terrorist people were contemplating plan to carry terrorist activities in province of Ontario and the targets were located in city of Toronto, and city of Ottawa. The seventeen terrorist planned to claim the Honorable Prime Minister of Canada HARPER's life.

How were these seventeen men recruited? Who did finance the seventeen men to train with explosive and to purchase explosive? Were the Mullahs behind the threat? Will the CSIS and RCMP be able to apprehended terrorist people prior to their attack?

The United Nation {U.N.} is aware of Human Right Violations in Iran and is doing nothing to stop Human Rights Violations in Iran. The United Nation is turned in some kind of boys club, and for the U.N. members simply they enjoy excellent quality of life and to make a few business deals at a given opportunity, which is a case for oil for food and when Annan was questioned, "Me: Regarding Oil for Food, you have said that you do not believe Security Council votes "were bought" by Saddam's contracts. Do you believe that billion of dollars that his regime granted to France and Russia through the program or through the oil allocations influenced their policies and stances against the resulting war? Do you think economic interests influence policies of member states? Annan: No comment. Me: What do you think are the lessons of what went wrong in the oil for Food program, in the sense that sanctions were busted and Iraqi regime was able to manipulate the will and efforts of the international community for its own means? Annan: No comment".[117] Simply, Annan was speechless. The U.N is nothing but a social club, and referring to some of their poor management skills; "the U.N. was billed $123,844.50 by a Baghdad restaurant to feed Iraqi government guards for 2003, despite the fact that there was a war and U.N. operations had been scaled back. Why was the U.N. footing the bill for Iraqi government employees anyway? In the end, the U.N. could not even confirm how much food was actually delivered or to whom...the U.N. overpaid by $622,893 for voice, fax and communication services".[118] The security level of the U.N. "could not keep track of private phone calls placed on U.N. satellite phones".[119]

Iran's contemporary Herodotus:

Herodotus was born sometimes in 490 BC in Halicarnassus, Herodotus is well known figure as Father of History for West. He wrote about ancient Iran's history with respect to Achaemenid dynasty. Today, there are historian scholars who found bias in Herodotus recording ancient Iran's history. The scholars claimed that Herodotus recorded history from beneficial point for Greek. Today in Iran's contemporary history is not any different than past. Today, there are several Herodotus who sought to record Mullah's History as a benevolent one. There are two individuals who are caught red handed as they are portraying a picture of Mullah as benevolent. One is Dr. Roy MOTTAHEDEH and Dr. Noam CHOMSKY. They illustrated Mullah as if the Mullah is cherished by Iranians. However, bringing forward evidence from their own work and prove otherwise.

When there is a dictator and there is a Herodotus in order to smooth and soften road for the dictator. Dr. Roy MOTTAHEDEH in his book "The Mantle of the Prophet" illustrated Khomeini as a wonderful person and who brought positive changes in Iran. According to Dr. MOTTAHEDEH; "Khomeini might have had contacts with British imperialism or because he wrote erotic poetry under pseudonym "The Indian." (Khomeini's grandfather was a Kashmiri sayyed of Iranian origin, and Khomeini had name "The Indian" for his *erfani* poetry.)"[120] Interestingly, MOTTAHEDEH did not deny that Khomeini had contact with Britain, and he was an agent of Britain. MOTTAHEDEH tried to justify Khomeini's association with British and wrote that Khomeini used "The Indian" as a PEN name because he would write "erotic poetry". Khomeini never wrote poetry, and his religious guideline was about how to have sex with a minor and not to be held responsible for his crime, so if anyone would think having a sex with a minor was erotic, it is really interesting. Plus, Khomeini was not Sufi either, Mullah's do not like Sufi and consider Sufi as an infidel. According to MOTTAHEDEH, Khomeini's grandfather was *Sayyed* of Iranian origin. The word *Sayyed* is an Arabic word which means Mr. Persian word for Mr. is *Agha*. Khomeini's grand father was an <u>Arab Bedouins</u> who left their desert and went for looting other nations, and taking booty. Khomeini was not Iranian whatsoever period. There is also imperative factor of geographic; Kashimir is located between Pakistan and India. Iran does not have a border with India. Natural conclusion, MOTTAHEDEH is manipulating readers mind by providing misinformation.

According to Dr. MOTTAHEDEH; "Khomeini, while under arrest, sent out a proclamation that the wealthy should help the poor; and, in fact, some wealthy men of the bazaar did distribute charcoal and funds".[121] MOTTAHEDEH is correct that Khomeini instructed businessmen to support the revolution and the businessmen funded the revolution. There is this matter of charcoal. In Iran no one burn charcoal as mean to generate heat in their home, or cook food. In Iran, people do not use coal to generate heat either because price of oil is reasonable. The only time, in Iranian culture charcoal runs in the middle of living room when people are smoking opium which is known as *Vapoor* time. Dr. MOTTAHEDEH is making mistake with another occasion.

The Mullahs are proud of their background that they are Arabs and children of Prophet Muhammad, there is nothing wrong with it that they are children of Prophet Muhammad, Prophet Muhammad Peace Upon is a nice person, there is no queer on that. However, there is a serious problem with children of Muhammad, they think because they come from family line of Muhammad they have the right to do

what they want and justify their action as "famous saying of the Prophet
will be fulfilled: the likeness of the people of my family is the likeness of
the ark of Noah; the one who embarks on it is saved, and the one who
holds back from it will drown and sink." God willingly, he says, the ark
will appear before the water rises much higher".[122]

The two individuals are sitting on a bench they are children of
Prophet Muhammad from your left hand is Ahmad Khomeini's son and
your right hand person is Khomeini. Khomeini was sign of God, and
people would kiss his hand. People made an idol out of him, and truly
worship Khomeini like a god. Koran says; "Yet, they worship, beside
Allah, Thing for which no authority Has been sent down to them, And
of which they have (Really) no knowledge: For those that do wrong
There is no help". [123]

Khomeini sign of God and one of children of Prophet Muhammad
had established an Islamic state in Iran and "the regime Has executed
people for nonpolitical crimes such as drug trafficking, gambling,
homosexuality, prostitution, pimping, and adultery, as well as for
murder and rape, it has also executed people for political crimes like
spying, counterrevolution, and "sowing corruption on earth".[124] The
Mullahs are straight minded people and they know one simple language
which is to kill or not to kill, so the Mullahs kill anyone at any time,
and the Mullahs do not have rational and critical mind to manage
perplex country, the Mullahs cannot incorporate theology doctrine

into political, social and economic policies, the Mullahs are trained in field of theology which is not compatible with real life issues "the ex-cleric who told me about clerical training for example, had come to the conclusion that "clerics are nothing but shopkeepers' of religion," a parasite class. "They are alien to the real message and teaching of Islam, whose goal is the moral upbringing of people," he said. "All they do is fill up people's minds and hearts with rules that have no basis in the Koran and are based in false interpretations and substantiated tales." Clerics generally receive stipend from the government, from their followers, or from their mentors".[125]

The Mullahs brought Iran to a lowest point "the Mullahs Greatest Accomplishment, political serial killings in Iran, political oppression, oppression of religious minority, promotion of corruption, prostitution and drug addiction, stealing Iran's wealth and transferring the funds to overseas banks, destruction of Iran's economy, making Iran an international "embarrassment", broadcasting to the world Suicide TV, arbitrary arrests, interrogation under torture, no legal representation for those accused of crimes, and selling Iranian women as sex slaves in the United Arab Emirates"[126]there are more crimes against humanity committed by the Mullahs in Iran, the above criminal offences were simply some handful of them.

The Mullahs are justifying their criminal offences by inventing one new bureau to their judicial system of Mullah which is called *"Papoush"* {fabricating evidence against accused person in any shape or form} making department. Briefly examining the Mullah's *"Papoush"* system and how the Mullahs has committed tremendous crimes against Humanity and bringing forward one of surviving victim's testimony. Madam LATIFI's father was a military Colonel during reign of the King. The Iranian Immortal Solider, Honorable Colonel LATIFI was apprehended and incarcerated by the Mullah's hooligans. When the hooligans apprehended Immortal Honorable Colonel LATIFI, his wife did not know where was her husband? Eventually, wife found her husband at one of hooligan's jail. Immortal Honorable Colonel LATIFI was charged with offence of murdering people. Immortal Honorable Colonel LATIFI's wife provided evidences and proved that her husband was not involved with murdering anyone. However, the Mullahs had their own mind. When Immortal Honorable Colonel LATIFI was sitting in a judicial room his wife had observed," the words *Mofsed'e Fel Arz* (Corrupt of the Earth) had written on the blackboard".[127] {There are several pictures which prove that the detainees were forced to sit in a room and there was a blackboard, and on it was written corruptor of earth}. Therefore, Immortal Honorable Colonel LATIFI never had a fair trial; the Mullah judicial system never took into account presumed innocent until proven guilty. The Mullah judicial system was guilty until proven innocent. The Immortal Honorable Colonel LATIFI was guilty no matter what. {There is a question for Ms. Shirin EBADI, during her acceptance speech for her Noble Peace Prize she accused the U.S. for Human Rights Violation, than why does not she accuse the Mullahs for Human Rights Violation publicly? Oh I forgot, my mistake, she is too busy writing books, every year she writes about three books and who does write these books for her? }

Interestingly, newspaper wrote their own version of *"Papoush"* deformation of character for Immortal Honorable Colonel LATIFI's offence, the article wrote that," during course of revolutionary trial at Tehran, four individuals disclosed that the King and Ovisi {Ovisi was a General} had planned to plant land minds during course of Ashura ceremony}".[128] Immortal Honorable Colonel LATIFI could not plant land mines in street of Tehran and killing people, he had to dig the side walk and people could see him digging the cement side walk. The media was manipulating people's emotion that Immortal Honorable Colonel LATIFI was against grandson of Prophet Muhammad. The media was justifying the butcher shop of Khomeini.

The hooligans did not treat the Immortal Honorable Colonel LATIFI with respect and dignity. The hooligans broke his both wrists during interrogations. The hooligans tormented LATIFI family, and the hooligans were getting pleasure by tormenting distraught family. The hooligan engaged in psychologically war with her mother and was disturbing her every time and was saying that; "we will fetch your husband now," she was told... Waiting there, in that little classroom, it suddenly occurred to my mother that her children would also grow up without father. She bit her lip to keep from crying...Maybe this whole thing was a cruel joke; maybe the guards had simply found a new way to torment her and were outside".[129]

The Mullahs were murdering Iran's finest with intention to destroy Iran and Madam LATIFI's father was one of the Immortal that, "he stood tall and straight, the good soldier. And my mother knew in her heart, if not in her mind, that her husband of fourteen years, the only man she'd ever loved, was preparing to go to his death. That was the moment she fell apart. She turned to the guards, sobbing, and asked them how they could let this happen. Her husband was an honorable man. He had done nothing wrong. He had four children at home... They put the blindfold over her tearstained face, escorted her out, and walked her across the parking lot...Just as they reached it, a short rang out".[130]

Still, the family is in pain for loss of their beloved father, "Twenty-five years later, as I began writing this book, my mother broke down and remembered that terrible morning when she saw my cousin Nasser pulling up his car, looking devastated". [131] The Mullahs took the Immortal Honorable Colonel LATIFI from his family and the Immortal Honorable Colonel LATIFI and many more Iranian Immortal Soldiers like him were the people who kept the Middle East in peace and Western nations were sleeping in beauty at night under command of King of Kings Mohammad Reza PAHLAVI First.

Madam LATIFI mentioned that when she went back to Iran to visit her home she remembered, "... I was crying in earnest, and I felt my mother's hand reaching for mine. I could not stop crying. This was where my family had been torn apart. This was where my life had been interrupted". [132]Dr. CORSI was absolutely correct in his book "Atomic Iran" when he mentioned that the Mullah's greatest achievement was murdering people, and the Mullah's cannot be trusted with nuclear capability. Thus, a prudent person would come to natural conclusion that nuclear Mullahs would result to an inevitable pending mass murdering people and to have more families like Madam LATIFI, who would mourn to rest of their life.

Dr. Noam CHOMSKY has a doctoral in linguistic and does not have doctoral in Political Science. Dr. CHOMSKY was interviewed by Dr. Ramin JAHANBEGLOO, who had a doctoral in Political Science. CHOMSKY has a unique perspective on Iran's situation Dr. JAHANBEGLOO asked Dr. CHOMSKY; "Have you ever been to Iran? NC: No."[133] CHOMSKY never been in Iran, which means he never walked in a small village and shake hands with people, researching one of Iran's ethnic language and get to know their problems, concerns, needs and wants. Further in the interview, "RJ: Are you interested to go to Iran? NC: Yes, I have invitations I just have not been able to make it. I have an extremely intense schedule. I'm usually planned two years ahead, it is hard to working things out".[134] Dr. CHOMSKY mentioned that I have an extremely intense schedule. I'm usually planned two years ahead, it is hard to working things out, which means CHOMSKY cannot spare his time at will. There is this evidence which proves CHOMSKY has plenty of time in his hand, and can go to Iran for two weeks. On September 11th, 2001 Osama Bin-Laden masterminded a terrorist attack on U.S. soil, the terrorist attacked send a shock wave crossed nations. CHOMSKY took his sweet time and wrote a book with name of ". 9-11. NY, NY: A Seven Stories Press First Edition, 2001 which has 125 pages the size of the book is 5 cm to 7 cm." {This 9-11 book is sitting on my book shelf} if CHOMSKY has an extremely intense schedule, how did he manage to write the above book? CHOMSKY is lacking credibility, he is not trustworthy person. More from interview "RJ: When you think of a country like Iran, since you have never visited, what are your perceptions of Iran today? NC: Well, I have been interested in Iran since the early 1950s when the United States and Britain overthrow the conservative-nationalist government and restored the Shah. I have been following Iran throughout that whole period. I was involved with Iranian dissidents. Iranian students in the period of protest against the Shah and of course I have paid a lot of attention since the overthrow of the Shah when the Islamic regime took over. Most of what I look at is from the point of U.S. policy. So I have been interested in the role of Iran under the Shah as part of a system of control of Middle East oil and later as a partial antagonist. I read and follow what's happening. My picture now is pretty conventional. There is clearly now a **significant reform**".[135] CHOMSKY has a doctoral in linguistic, the King was not disposed, how CHOMSKY came to conclusion that the King was restored? And with respect to **significant reform** in Iran, on April 27th, 2006, Mullah's hooligan enforcers apprehended Dr. Ramin JAHANBEGLOO and Persian Journal indicated that; "Ramin Jahanbegloo has been linked to the CIA and the Mossad"[136] Dr. JAHANBEGLOO reject hand picked Mullah president, Mahmoud Ahmedinezhad that Holocaust did not occurred, JAHANBEGLOO wrote an article for Spanish newspaper El Pais and defended victim of Holocaust. Persian Journal; "the hardline paper argued that he had "obtained this Canadian citizenship to use in times of danger".[137] In 1993, he went back to Iran, and was a professor at the University of Tehran the Mullahs did not like his tone and was chased around by the hooligans because the hooligans did not like his moderate tone, he left Iran and he also did not have a good marriage. He left Iran in a good term. He worked at the University of Toronto in his field of political philosophy. In 2001, he returned to Iran to build Iran, regrettably the Mullahs did not like his voice of reason, and moderation. The Mullahs wanted war, crime, violence in order to remain in power and to resurrect their Hidden Imam from absent. "Given the fact that the Islamic Republic of Iran {Mullah} continues to pursue suspect nuclear program, having a leader with a messianic vision is no cause to rejoice".[138] Interestingly, the Holy Koran mentioned that Prophet Jesus will come and save the world from chaos and the Holy Koran never mentioned anything about hidden Imam.

Concept of Global Village versus MACHAIVELLI doctrine.

Marshall McLuhan defined concept of global village "refers to the immediate experience of sights and sounds from anywhere in the world when transmitted by electronic media". [139]

MACHIAVELLI believed a king could secure his captured kingdom by killing those who had closed association with the previous king, and those who had less associating with king could be spare their life. The new king could spare them by dispersing them around the world. Eventually, those dispersed around the world will naturalize to their new adopted home and would forget their past.

Iranian people inside of Iran and outside of Iran are fully aware of the Mullah's diabolic agenda which is all about world domination and destruction of civilization as we know. In summer of 1987, Mullah Khameini made it clear and crystal when he preached at people during Friday pray at University of Tehran that a "Muslim person won't be admitted in Allah's heaven, unless a person kills one American, one French, one German, one Israel, and one British citizen. Then, Allah would allow the person to enter the garden of heaven". The Iranian residing out side of Iran are fully aware of the pending danger of the fanatic Mullah and how cunning fox would be the Islamic Republic of Mullah which is "must" to collapse for world security and safety. The Iranians outside of Iran want to overthrow the theocracy state of the Mullah so their pending threat does not spread in the West, and the Western people not to have same bitter experience as the self-exile Iranians have. Iranians outside of Iran are in communication with Iranians inside of Iran via means of electronic equipments; such as, Internet. The Internet has expanded résistance frontier against the Islamic Republic of Mullah. The Mullahs have lost battle on Internet because there are many web sites and there are kinds of filter which has become impossible for the Mullahs to censor the Internet. Iranians outside of Iran are providing Iranians inside of Iran with tools and keys to defend their legal rights. Then, Iranians inside of Iran are transmitting Human Rights Violation evidences to the Iranians outside of Iran. The Iranians outside of Iran are acting as a special interest group and lobbying politicians and Humanitarian Organizations in order to stop Human Rights Violation in Iran.

When, there was no Internet Iranian people still did communicate with one another. During reign of Safavid dynasty citizens would go to coffee houses and engaged in hotly debates with respect to current social, political, economic, and religious issues as Dr. Babayan recorded from; "Chardin depicts the coffeehouse as a place where one could tune into the latest news and where political criticism was voiced in full liberty, free of government scrutiny, for the court was not concerned with what people said". [140] In sixteen century, Safavid dynasty, there was a freedom of speech and Iranians would gather in a coffee shop and would engage in a dialogue on daily issues. The coffee shop was acting as a source of information or today's Internet as Dr. NEWMAN mentioned that "as the coffee-house, open from dawn until late into the evenings, where people met to drink coffee or different sorts of cordials, smoke tobacco and opium and listen to recitations of poetry and stories and, relatively freely, discuss the affair of the day".[141] The coffee houses became sanctuaries for Iranian citizens to gather and to discuss current political issues without fear of retaliation from anyone. Eventually, the Safavid Kings decided to take part with their citizens and to develop close relation with their citizens and to learn first hand account with regard to their citizens needs and wants, the Kings would enter in the coffee houses and engaged in discussion with their citizens .[142]

In 2538/1979 revolution, coffee houses did play a role for revolution at city of Tabriz Province of Azarbijon, there was a coffee shop with name of "Jackass Coffee House" "*eshak lar ghafase*", in district of "*darbe chaki*" Chalk Door. This above mentioned coffee house had its own distinct patrons, who would engage in the most rude and unpleasant joke with one anther. The patrons were involved in revolution and were making plan how to cause riot in city of Tabriz. Also, city of Tabriz is an epicenter for revolution in Iran. Once, people of Azerbijon would revolt against the state, the authority would have a difficult time to deal with them, and other provinces would join with Azerbijon uprising and the state would not be able to contain the turmoil. After revolution these certain patrons of this "Jackass Coffee House" hold important post as a Revolutionary Guards at city of Tabriz.

In seventeen century, in Europe, the coffee houses had functioned as gathering places for citizens to engage in political discussion. The coffee houses would motivate people to discuss about their issues and not to feel indifferent about their country's concern. This coffee houses made people self aware about their current issues, and made people to become self-less which lead to French-Revolution.

Today, Iranian people do not go to coffee shop to discuss their current political issues with one another. Today, Iranian people sit at comfort of their home and are watching television programs or watching a programs on their monitor of their computer that the programs are running and managed by certain individuals who are charismatic anchors; such as, Mr. Behrouz SOURESRAFIL, or Madam Haleh NAZERI, there television studio is located in the United State of America and their programs are zooming in Iran and outside of Iran. They educated Iranians outside of Iran and inside of Iran with respect to their problems and not allowing the Mullahs to get away from their horrible crimes. Now, the coffee houses are transformed into individual house and a television set. These anchors won't be able to do revolution or ousting the Islamic Republic of Mullah, but the anchors are an instrument to educate Iranians outside of Iran and inside of Iran with regard to injustice which is occurring daily to them by the Mullahs who are blood thirsty. Mr. Behrouz SOURSRAFIL and Madam Haleh NAZERI were successful to defuse Mohsen SAZEGARA {ops sorry, Dr. Mohsen SAZEGARA, he also has doctoral. King of Kings Mohammad Reza PAHLAVI's advisors were technocrat, and could speak several foreign languages, and these hooligans wanted to state that they are intellectuals.}, who was one of hooligan during revolution, and during post revolution he had several key posts, one post was from Iran's intelligent bureau. Dr. SAZEGARA claimed that he repented and wanted to join Iranian people, and he had an idea to oust the Mullahs from Iran. Dr. SAZEGARA wanted to have a referendum in Iran. Dr. SAZEGARA deemed that Iranians were naïve and could fool them and would buy his story and the Mullah's state would be dragged for sometimes in peace. Dr. SAZEGARA wanted to have a referendum on Iran's constitutional law. Interestingly, Khameini sign of god and other Mullahs are representative of god on earth has final word on anything, and how this referendum would alter the Mullah's political dynamic? There is one political party which is selected by supreme leader Khameini. Mr. SOURESRAFIL and Madam NAZERI exposed Dr. SAZEGARA's identity and could not do much. They closed his referendum door for good.

There was one interesting point about this Dr. SAZEGARA that he was chanting death to U.S. at time when he was in Iran and now he is residing in U.S., and he claimed that he was incarcerated for one hundred and fourteen days for his political view. In Iran, if anyone incarcerated in jail, they will remain in jail for minimum of fifteen years, or accidentally they die! How come, Dr. SAZEGARA did not serve fifteen years of jail terms? How come he converted to secularism in year 2001 when President Bush decided to spread democracy around the world and Iran was an axis of evil? And Dr. SAZEGARA was from intelligent bureau who was converted to secularism?

Iranians are using modern and advance communication tools to make contact with Iranian outside of Iran and inside of Iran. Madam Nazanin AFSHIN-JAM, Iranian-Canadian, the 2003 Miss World became aware that there was an Iranian-Kurdish lady in Iran with name of Nazanin FATEHI, who was in a death row. Madam AFSHIN launched her campaign to save Nazanin FATEHI from absolute death, and caused awareness with respect to gross Human Rights Violation in Iran.

Madam FATEHI was confronted by a man and wanted to sexually assault her and her niece. Madam FATEHI and her niece commenced to flee, and Madam FATEHI was carrying a small knife with herself, and the bad guy attacked at Madam FATEHI and her niece with intention to sexually assault them. Madam FATEHI as a last course of resource for her self-preservation and her self-defence, when the culprit made a physical confrontation with her, she stabbed the culprit on his hand. Madam FATEHI ran for her safety again. However, the culprit pursued her and he was illustrating aggression to her and the culprit was able to take down Madam FATEHI. Then, Madam FATEHI wanted to push away the culprit off herself, while she was struggling for her life and her niece safety, her visual and audio were shut down due to fear, Madam FATEHI unintentionally caused the culprit to lose his life with one fatal stab. The Mullah court passed a disposition of death sentence for her. According to children of Prophet Muhammad, women are evils and are causing men to attack at them. Therefore, men are innocent victims of women's seduction. Apparently, women are seducing men to rape women. How creative is the Mullah's mind?

On Wednesday May 31ˢᵗ, 2006 Nazanin AFSHIN-JAM made front page of the Globe and Mail, and educated Iranian-Canadians and other Canadians with respect to whole range of Human Rights abuses which are taking place in Iran by the culprit of Mullahs. Madam AFSHIN ran an online petition and collected signatures from people online in order to stop the Mullahs from murdering Madam FATEHI. Madam AFSHIN used Internet in her mission in order to reach to generation that they are using Internet http://www.bodogmusic.com/artists/nazanin.php . Eventually, she collected sufficient signatures and stopped the Mullahs from murdering Madam FATEHI. Currently, there is an appeal for Madam FATEHI case. The above example illustrated how Iranians outside of Iran were organizing themselves and defending Iranians inside of Iran.{I would display Madam AFSHIN picture, but everyone would be distract due her to beauty}.

There are special interest groups {SIG} outside of Iran; such as, Iran of Tomorrow Movement or known as www.sosiran.com is located in the United State of America and it is in touch with Iranians who are residing out side of Iran and inside of Iran. This special interest group is running television programs on Internet and on television. There is an anchor person with name of Dr. Iman FOROUTAN, who is exposing the Islamic Republic of Mullah's corruption and Human Rights Violation from valid source of information that they are the Iranian non-governmental organizations {NGO}. These NGOs are contacting the television programs and providing account of gross Human Rights Violation in Iran. This Special Interest Group was successful to give courage and logical reason to Iranian people inside of Iran to come out of their home and to celebrate Iran's culture particularly *Cha Har Shanbeh Sore*. Iranian listened to Dr. Iman FOROUTAN and despised the Mullahs because the Mullahs did not like Iranian culture and would imprison anyone to cherish Iranian culture. This Special Interest Group obtained two video tapes from fanatic Muslims in Iran, and there was one hooligan with name of "yes" he has Dr. too he is Dr. ABBASI {he has doctoral too, and Iran's president Mahmoud Ahmedi Nezhad has doctoral too} that how terrorism was divine and he was terrorist and trained terrorist individuals to combat Zionists.

There is one more Special Interest Group which is directed by Mr. Khaleghi Yazdi, he calls his Special Interest Group Hakha Movement http://www.ahura.info/ who is promoting Iranian identity and he is trying to revive Iranian nationalism, which is an excellent weapon to defend Iranian people against Arab Bedouins invader of Iran. There are people inside of Iran and out side of Iran who are watching his television programs and are listening to him carefully for what he says. When he asks Iranian people inside of Iran to come out peacefully, Iranian people do listen to him and come out of their home. Mr. Khalegi Yazdi needs to coordinate his agenda with other Special Interest Groups in order to have optimal result. Mr. Khalegi Yazdi was first front runner when National Geographic was abusing name of Persian Gulf, he was encouraging people to write letters to the National Geographic to stop abusing Persian Gulf name.

The National Geographic decided to abuse Persian Gulf name and Iranian out side of Iran decided to defend Iran's identity and establish Persian Gulf Task Force http://www.persiangulfonline.org/ the Persian Gulf Task Force began to investigate those organizations that they were abusing Persian Gulf name and is in contact with Iranian globally via Internet. The Persian Gulf Task Force decided to cause awareness by selling Persian Gulf Wrist Band. The Persian Gulf Task Force gained popularity among Iranian particularly during first day of spring as Iranian celebrates New Year and the Persian Gulf Task Force organizes New Year celebration at city of New York.

Madam Ladan and Madam Roya Boroumand their beloved father Dr. Abdorrahman Boroumand was murdered by the Mullahs. On April 18th, 1991 the Mullahs assassinated Dr. Boroumand in Paris. Ladan and Roya with assistant of Reza Nassehi established a foundation for Dr. Abdorrahman Boroumand. This foundation has no political affiliation with anyone and this foundation is non-governmental. The foundation is protecting and promoting Human Rights in Iran http://www.abfiran. org/. The foundation has a database which is collecting data that how the Islamic Republic of Mullah is violating Human Rights in Iran. Obviously, once the theology state of the Mullahs collapse, these collected data will be use against the culprits.

In conclusion, the above web sites were sample of efforts of Iranian people to remain in touch with Iranian people inside of Iran and outside of Iran. The electronic equipments brought Iranians closer together and creating Iranian solidarity regardless of one's cultural background. The MACHIAVELLI doctrine that dispersing those who are less associated with the king failed by today's standard. People can get connected with their motherland and assist one another in order to oust a dictator state because today we are living in a global village.

This dictator of Arab Bedouins has altered Iran's political culture "is the result of the interplay of historic and contemporary factors in an ongoing process of socialization from childhood through adulthood. It may contain subsets, or subcultures, based on ethnic, geographic, and class difference".[143] Iranian people do not have Safavid dynasty as their political culture, now Iranian people call themselves Persian and want to be related to glorious of Persia. The Iranian citizens had experienced with the Pahlavi Monarchy, and Iran was moving toward its pinnacle point. Crown Prince Reza PAHLAVI Heir to Throne of Iran has knowledge and courage to move Iran toward glorious time of Persia under capacity of Constitutional Monarchy if Iranian people want.

The Constitutional Monarchy is best form of government which works in Iran because people have Republic state too. People are voting for a candidate to become a prime minister of Iran and there is a king or queen who is overseeing political activities in Iran. The king or queen has no political advantage but is seeking well being of his/her citizens and a king or queen has no political interest to be reelected to office. The Constitutional Monarchy diminishes power of politics and distributes power among political parties and political parties are representing people's interest and power is transform into accountability and responsibility of people in parliament, and no one is in absolute power position. In case, of Republic state one person possesses political power and power leads to corruptions.

This Constitutional Monarchy was as old as Republic State which history has recorded at the time of King of Kings Xerxes during battle of Salamis, when the King was planning to launch an attack on Greek; the King was using his council. On the other hand, Greece was a Republic and one council was deciding how to manage affair of the war which was all about cheating on Greek people.

The Constitutional Monarchy is not a suitable state for a country that the country was librated from hands of colonizer. In this case, librated people have bitter taste of monarchy and would move toward Republic state.

Before selection, Standing beside her significant of other, heavy make-up, showing off her hair, nice bright colorful scarf, and of course she is merely drinking juice and nothing in it. Coming to this focal point that do Iranian people write in English language? Do Iranian people go to polling station and read English on ballot sheet? I wonder why

Hashme is spelled in English and not Persian! Was election for Iranian or U.S.? Life is great just for hooligans and Mullahs. Please do not stop drinking your booze [French for drinking, did not mean your alcohol beverage, Mullahs and hooligans are saints and do not do anything bad, god forgive, they are god's *Sayyed*].

On June 12th, 2006 Iranian women came out for peaceful assembly and asking for equal right. The Mullah responded with Iron fist.

"Conclusion"

Every story must have happy ending, and this story does not have happy ending. Still, the Mullahs are in Iran and robbing Iranian people's wealth and stashing Iranian people's money in a foreign banks or investing it overseas. The Iranian people want to have a stable state {Constitutional Monarchy or a Republic State}, the state is not monopolizing power but power is diminished in hands of people and state is acting according to Constitutional Law. There are political parties and people go to polling station and are voting for their favorite political parties and majority elected party establish a government for next four years. Iranians want to have a government that does not have power but it has responsibility as well as accountability toward its citizen and not subject. The Iranians want to express their thought and criticize the political parties and they cannot. Therefore, "the Islamic Republic of Iran is not Saddam Hussein's Iraq. A fragile civil society has been allowed to survive the brutal dictatorship of the mullahs. Students, journalists, lawyers, businessmen, and others have created pockets of resistance".[144] There is a happy ending story which is looming like a sun at horizon for Iranians.

This book would have a conclusion by readers help. When a reader of this book to say viva United Eternal Iran in their own ethnic language. Viva Iran, Payendeh bad Iran, Yasha Iran, or how do you say viva Iran in your language? Say it and mean it.

Final notes, why the term children of Prophet Muhammad was used? Because the Mullahs or *Seyyad* were calling themselves children of Prophet Muhammad and they were seeking respect and obedience from Iranians. Therefore, there was no intention to disrespect faith of Islam and simply captured tone of the Mullahs.

This book was scheduled to be published year 2007. However, this book is published 2006 because currently there are sporadic uprisings from each corner of Iran particularly city of Tabriz is an epicenter for revolution in Iran and on June 03rd, 2006 People of Tabriz defied the theology state and all Iranian people are defying the Mullahs at every given opportunity. Therefore, this book is rushed to the publisher and there was an insufficient time to polish the manuscript because Iranian people need to know one fact straight and that not to trust any children of Prophet Muhammad, and liberate Iran with their own effort and with leadership of Crown Prince Reza PAHLAVI as well as the council who are true to Iran. At the end, power and glory will be for Iranian people.

The pictures were displayed in order to prove beyond reasonable a doubt that the Mullahs were, are and will be cold blood murderer and Human Right Abusers and there was no deformation of character. Also, with regard to some pictures accused people have clear mug shots, so it will be use against them in future International Tribunal while accused people were committing crime against Humanity.

The author of this book acted in good faith at all time and brought forward articles and materials which were available in public domain.

If Iran Does not Exist, I Do not Exist, Ferdowsi

End Notes

[1] Babayan, Kathryn. <u>Mystics, Monarchs, and Messiahs</u>. Harvard University: Harvard University Press, 2002, pg446.

[2] Jahed, Reza. <u>Ghanjhae Manavi</u>. Mash had, fall of 1377. pg 266. ISBN 964-6550-20-7

[3] Salehpour, Salehe. <u>Divan Hafez.</u> Tehran, Iran: Booteh Press, 1998, page 144. ISBN 964-90021-5-4

[4] Abdullah Yusuf Ali. <u>The Meaning of Holy Qu, ran</u>. Beltsville Maryland US: Amana Publisher, 1997pg 853.

[5] Bondanella, Peter, and Mark Musa. <u>The Portable MACHIAVELLI</u>. T.O ON: Penguin Books Canada Ltd, 1979. pg35.

[6] Newman J. Andrew. <u>Safavid Iran: Rebirth of a Persian Empire</u>. NY, NY: I.B. Tauris & Co Ltd., 2006, pg18.

[7] Newman J. Andrew. <u>Safavid Iran: Rebirth of a Persian Empire</u>. NY, NY: I.B. Tauris & Co Ltd., 2006, pg15.

[8] Bondanella, Peter, and Mark Musa. <u>The Portable MACHIAVELLI</u>. T.O ON: Penguin Books Canada Ltd, 1979. pg 80.

[9] King of Kings PAHLAVI, Mohammad Reza. <u>Answer to History.</u> Briarcliff Manor, N.Y: Scarborough House, 1980. pg 104.

[10] King of Kings PAHLAVI, Mohammad Reza. <u>Answer to History.</u> Briarcliff Manor, N.Y: Scarborough House, 1980. pg 104.

[11] Mathewson Denny, Frederick. <u>An Introduction to Islam</u>. Englewood Cliffs, NJ: Macmillan Publishing Company, 1985. pg 107.

[12] Abdullah Yusuf Ali. <u>The Meaning of Holy Quran</u>. Beltsville Maryland US: Amana Publisher, 1997, pg 1238.

[13] King of Kings PAHLAVI, Mohammad Reza. <u>Answer to History.</u> Briarcliff Manor, N.Y: Scarborough House, 1980. pg 59.

[14] King of Kings PAHLAVI, Mohammad Reza. <u>Answer to History.</u> Briarcliff Manor, N.Y: Scarborough House, 1980.pg 149.

[15] Alavi, Nasrin. <u>We Are Iran: The Persian Blogs</u>. Brooklyn NY: Soft Skull Press, Inc., 2005. pg146.

[16] King of Kings PAHLAVI, Mohammad Reza. <u>Answer to History.</u> Briarcliff Manor, N.Y: Scarborough House, 1980.pg 149.

[17] <u>http://www.frontpagemag.com/Article/Printable.asp?ID=20780</u> Feb 12th, 2006.

[18] http://www.frontpagemag.com/Article/Printable.ansp?ID=20780 Feb 12th, 2006.

[19] Ganji, Manouchehr. Defying the Iranian: Revolution From a Minister to the Shah to a Leader of Resistance. U.S.A: Praeger Publisher: 2002. pg27.

[20] King of Kings PAHLAVI, Mohammad Reza. Answer to History. Briarcliff Manor, N.Y: Scarborough House, 1980.pg 172.

[21] http://www.mihanam.com/Pages/Islam/Khomaini_1.htm. May 22nd, 2006

[22] SMCCDI

[23] Bondanella, Peter, and Mark Musa. The Portable MACHIAVELLI. T.O ON: Penguin Books Canada Ltd, 1979. pg 135.

[24] King of Kings PAHLAVI, Mohammad Reza. Answer to History. Briarcliff Manor, N.Y: Scarborough House, 1980.pg 184.

[25] Milani, Abbas. The Persian Sphinx: Amir Abbas Hoveyda and the Riddle of the Iranian Revolution. Washington DC: Mage Publisher, 2000-2004, pg24.

[26] Milani, Abbas. The Persian Sphinx: Amir Abbas Hoveyda and the Riddle of the Iranian Revolution. Washington DC: Mage Publisher, 2000-2004, pg 26.

[27] King of Kings PAHLAVI, Mohammad Reza. Answer to History. Briarcliff Manor, N.Y: Scarborough House, 1980.pg 184.

[28] GHAFFARI, Mahmoud. Top gunned down. Iranian.com. July 22nd, 2004.

[29] GHAFFARi, Mahmoud. Top gunned down, Iranian.com. July 22nd, 2004.

[30] Bondanella, Peter, and Mark Musa. The Portable MACHIAVELLI. T.O ON: Penguin Books Canada Ltd, 1979. pg 80.

[31] Berman, Marshall. All That Is Solid Melts Into Air. T.O ON: Penguin Books Canada Ltd, 1988. pg 78.

[32] Marx, Karl and Frederick Engles. The Communist Manifesto. Printed In The U.S: International Publisher Co., Inc., 1948.pg 29.

[33] Complied by Karim Emami, Zamineh Publisher, Tehran, 1979.

[34] King of Kings PAHLAVI, Mohammad Reza. Answer to History. Briarcliff Manor, N.Y: Scarborough House, 1980.pg 145.

[35] King of Kings PAHLAVI, Mohammad Reza. Answer to History. Briarcliff Manor, N.Y: Scarborough House, 1980.pg 145.

[36] Mottahedeh, Roy. The Mantle of the Prophet: Religion and Politics in Iran.185 Banbury Rd. Oxford UK: Oneworld Publications. 1985-2000, pg389-390

37 Bondanella, Peter, and Mark Musa. The Portable MACHIAVELLI. T.O ON: Penguin Books Canada Ltd, 1979. pg 131.

38 www.mehr.org/massacre_1988.htm May 25th, 2005.

39 www.mehr.org/massacre_1988.htm May 25th, 2005.

40 www.mehr.org/massacre_1988.htm May 25th, 2005.

41 www.mehr.org/massacre_1988.htm May 25th, 2005.

42 Bondanella, Peter, and Mark Musa. The Portable MACHIAVELLI. T.O ON: Penguin Books Canada Ltd, 1979. pg 134.

43 Dr. Abd Al-Husain Zarrinkuh. The Cambridge History of Iran. Cambridge UK: Cambridge University Press, 1995, pg 1.

44 Dr. Abd Al-Husain Zarrinkuh. The Cambridge History of Iran. Cambridge UK: Cambridge University Press, 1995, pg 1.

45 Dr. Abd Al-Husain Zarrinkuh. The Cambridge History of Iran. Cambridge UK: Cambridge University Press, 1995, pg 4-5.

46 Babayan, Kathryn. Mystics, Monarch, and Messiahs. Harvard University: Harvard University Press, 2002. pg 125.

47 Mathewson Denny, Frederick. An Introduction to Islam. Englewood Cliffs, NJ: Macmillan Publishing Company, 1985. pg 107

48 Prevas, John. Envy Of The Gods. Cambridge Center, Cambridge: Da Capo Press, 2004, pg8.

49 Ladjevardian, Reza. From Ancient Persia to Contemporary Iran. Washington DC: Mage Publisher.

50 Babaie Sussan and Kathryn Babayan. Slaves of The Shah: New Elite of Safavid Iran. New York, NY: I.B. Tauris & Co Ltd., 2004. pg 20.

51 Bondanella, Peter, and Mark Musa. The Portable MACHIAVELLI. T.O ON: Penguin Books Canada Ltd, 1979. pg 107.

52 Bondanella, Peter, and Mark Musa. The Portable MACHIAVELLI. T.O ON: Penguin Books Canada Ltd, 1979. pg 106.

53 Bondanella, Peter, and Mark Musa. The Portable MACHIAVELLI. T.O ON: Penguin Books Canada Ltd, 1979. pg 87.

54 Ghani, Cyrus. Iran and the Rise of Reza Shah: From Qajar Collapse to Pahalvi Power. NY, NY: I.B. Tauris, 1998-2000, pg179.

55 Ghani, Cyrus. Iran and the Rise of Reza Shah: From Qajar Collapse to Pahalvi Power. NY, NY: I.B. Tauris, 1998-2000, pg406.

56 Ghani, Cyrus. Iran and the Rise of Reza Shah: From Qajar Collapse to Pahalvi Power. NY, NY: I.B. Tauris, 1998-2000, pg406.

57 Ghani, Cyrus. Iran and the Rise of Reza Shah: From Qajar Collapse to Pahalvi Power. NY, NY: I.B. Tauris, 1998-2000, pg407.

[58] Kinzer, Stephen. All The Shah's Men: An American Coup and Roots of Middle East Terror. Hoboken, New Jersey: John Wiley & Sons Inc., 2003, pg166.

[59] Kinzer, Stephen. All The Shah's Men: An American Coup and Roots of Middle East Terror. Hoboken, New Jersey: John Wiley & Sons Inc., 2003, pg168.

[60] Hoveyda, Fereydoun. The Shah and The Ayatollah. Westport, CT: Praeger Publishers, 2003, pg 100.

[61] Brym, Robert. New Society. T.O ON: Harcourt Brace, 1995, pg 18.20

[62] Abisaad, Rula Jurdi. Converting Persia: Religion and Power in the Safavid Empire. New York, NY: I.B. Tauris, 2004, pg 11.

[63] Newman J. Andrew. Safavid Iran: Rebirth of a Persian Empire. NY, NY: I.B. Tauris & Co Ltd., 2006, pg45.

[64] Babayan, Kathryn. Mystics, Monarchs, and Messiahs. Harvard University: Harvard University Press, 2002, pg76.

[65] Abisaad, Rula Jurdi. Converting Persia: Religion and Power in the Safavid Empire. New York, NY: I.B. Tauris, 2004, pg 30.

[66] Abisaad, Rula Jurdi. Converting Persia: Religion and Power in the Safavid Empire. New York, NY: I.B. Tauris, 2004, pg 21.

[67] Abisaad, Rula Jurdi. Converting Persia: Religion and Power in the Safavid Empire. New York, NY: I.B. Tauris, 2004, pg36.

[68] Abisaad, Rula Jurdi. Converting Persia: Religion and Power in the Safavid Empire. New York, NY: I.B. Tauris, 2004, pg36.

[69] Abisaad, Rula Jurdi. Converting Persia: Religion and Power in the Safavid Empire. New York, NY: I.B. Tauris, 2004, pg112.

[70] Abisaad, Rula Jurdi. Converting Persia: Religion and Power in the Safavid Empire. New York, NY: I.B. Tauris, 2004, pg99.

[71] Abisaad, Rula Jurdi. Converting Persia: Religion and Power in the Safavid Empire. New York, NY: I.B. Tauris, 2004, pg99.

[72] Babayan, Kathryn. Mystics, Monarchs, and Messiahs. Harvard University: Harvard University Press, 2002, pg21.

[73] Babayan, Kathryn. Mystics, Monarchs, and Messiahs. Harvard University: Harvard University Press, 2002, pg27.

[74] Rudolph P. Matthee and David Morgan. The Politics of Trade in Safavid Iran: Silk for Silver 1600-1730. Cambridge University: Cambridge University Press, 1999.

[75] Newman J. Andrew. Safavid Iran: Rebirth of a Persian Empire. NY, NY: I.B. Tauris & Co Ltd., 2006, pg102-103.

[76] Babayan, Kathryn. Mystics, Monarchs, and Messiahs. Harvard University: Harvard University Press, 2002, pg371.

[77] Ganji Manouchehr. Defying The Iranian Revolution: From a Minister

to the Shah to a Leader of Resistance. Westport, CT: Greenwood Publishing Group Inc., 2002, pg xix.

[78] Pahlavi, Mohammad Reza. The White Revolution of Iran . Kayhan Press. Pg iii.

[79] Lajevardi, Habib. Memoirs of Shapur Bakhtiar . Georgetwon Rd: Harvard University, 1996, pg 70. ISBN0-932885-14-4.

[80] Pahlavi, Mohammad Reza. The White Revolution of Iran . Kayhan Press. Pg86.

[81] Pahlavi, Mohammad Reza. The White Revolution of Iran . Kayhan Press. Pg94.

[82] Pahlavi, Mohammad Reza. The White Revolution of Iran . Kayhan Press. Pg96-97.

[83] Bondanella, Peter, and Mark Musa. The Portable MACHIAVELLI. T.O ON: Penguin Books Canada Ltd, 1979. pg 169.

[84] Bondanella, Peter, and Mark Musa. The Portable MACHIAVELLI. T.O ON: Penguin Books Canada Ltd, 1979. pg 135.

[85] PAHLAVI Mohammad Reza. Mission for my Country. T.O ON: McGRAW-HILL Book Company, Inc.1961,pg243.

[86] PAHLAVI Mohammad Reza. Mission for my Country. T.O ON: McGRAW-HILL Book Company, Inc.1961,pg235.

[87] PAHLAVI Mohammad Reza. Mission for my Country. T.O ON: McGRAW-HILL Book Company, Inc.1961, pg57.

[88] Anseri, M, Ali. Modern Iran Since 1921: The Pahlavis and After. Associated Companies throughout the world: Pearson Education Ltd., 2003, pg135.

[89] Anseri, M, Ali. Modern Iran Since 1921: The Pahlavis and After. Associated Companies throughout the world: Pearson Education Ltd., 2003, pg182.

[90] Ganji Manouchehr. Defying The Iranian Revolution: From a Minister to the Shah to a Leader of Resistance. Westport, CT: Greenwood Publishing Group Inc., 2002, pg xvi.

[91] PAHLAVI Mohammad Reza. Mission for my Country. T.O ON: McGRAW-HILL Book Company, Inc.1961,pg205.

[92] PAHLAVI Mohammad Reza. Mission for my Country. T.O ON: McGRAW-HILL Book Company, Inc.1961,pg287.

[93] Ganji Manouchehr. Defying The Iranian Revolution: From a Minister to the Shah to a Leader of Resistance. Westport, CT: Greenwood Publishing Group Inc., 2002, pg xx.

[94] King of Kings PAHLAVI, Mohammad Reza. Answer to History. Briarcliff Manor, N.Y: Scarborough House, pg 97.

[95] Bondanella, Peter, and Mark Musa. The Portable MACHIAVELLI. T.O ON: Penguin Books Canada Ltd, 1979. pg 199.

[96] Molavi, Afshin. The Soul of Iran. NY, NY: University Press of America, 2002, pg 17.

[97] Sens Allen and Peter Stoett. Global Politics: Origins, Currents, Directions. NY, NY: International Thomson Publishing, 1998, pg 62.

[98] Anseri, M, Ali. Modern Iran Since 1921: The Pahlavis and After. Associated Companies throughout the world: Pearson Education Ltd., 2003, pg137.

[99] Ganji Manouchehr. Defying The Iranian Revolution: From a Minister to the Shah to a Leader of Resistance. Westport, CT: Greenwood Publishing Group Inc., 2002, pg xxi.

[100] Babayan, Kathryn. Mystics, Monarchs, and Messiahs. Harvard University: Harvard University Press, 2002,pg 23.

[101] http://iranian.ws/iran_news/publish/printer_11430.shtml 10th, Dec 2005

[102] http://www.forbes.com/forbes/2003/0721/056_print.html 21st, July 2003.

[103] http://www.forbes.com/forbes/2003/0721/056_print.html 21st, July 2003.

[104] http://www.forbes.com/forbes/2003/0721/056_print.html 21st, July 2003.

[105] http://www.forbes.com/forbes/2003/0721/056_print.html 21st, July 2003.

[106] Alavi, Nasrin. We Are Iran: The Persian Blogs. Brooklyn, NY: Soft Skull Press Inc, 2005, pg148.

[107] http://www.forbes.com/forbes/2003/0721/056_print.html 21st, July 2003.

[108] http://www.forbes.com/forbes/2003/0721/056_print.html 21st, July 2003.

[109] Alavi, Nasrin. We Are Iran: The Persian Blogs. Brooklyn, NY: Soft Skull Press Inc, 2005, pg147.

[110] Kornbluh Peter, and Malcolm Byrne. The Iran-Contra Scandal: The Declassified History. NY, NY: The New Press, 1993, pg 380.

[111] King of Kings PAHLAVI, Mohammad Reza. Answer to History. Briarcliff Manor, N.Y: Scarborough House, 1980.pg 18.

[112] The Globe and Mail, March 31st, 2005.

[113] http://www.cbc./story/canada/national/2005/04/01/iranofficial-050401.html?print April 01st, 2005

[114] http://www.cbc./story/canada/national/2005/04/01/iranofficial-050401.html?print April 01st, 2005

[115] http://www.cbc./story/canada/national/2005/04/01/iranofficial-050401.html?print April 01st, 2005

[116] http://68onews.com/news/international/article.jsp?content=w031108A March 11th, 2005

[117] Shawn Eric. The U.N. Exposed. NY, NY: Penguin Book Published, 2006, pg 160.

[118] Shawn Eric. The U.N. Exposed. NY, NY: Penguin Book Published, 2006, pg 184.

[119] Shawn Eric. The U.N. Exposed. NY, NY: Penguin Book Published, 2006, pg 185.

[120] Mottahedeh, Roy. The Mantel of the Prophet. Oxford UK: Oneworld Publications, 1985-2000, pg372.

[121] Mottahedeh, Roy. The Mantel of the Prophet. Oxford UK: Oneworld Publications, 1985-2000, pg352.

[122] Mottahedeh, Roy. The Mantel of the Prophet. Oxford UK: Oneworld Publications, 1985-2000, pg390.

[123] Abdullah: Amana Publisher, 1997.pg Yusuf Ali. The Meaning of Holy Quran. Beltsville Maryland US, pg 840.

[124] Sciolino, Elaine. Persian Mirrors. NY, NY: Simon &Schuster, Inc., 2000, pg237.

[125] Sciolino, Elaine. Persian Mirrors. NY, NY: Simon &Schuster, Inc.,2000, pg199.

[126] Corsi R. Jerome. Atomic Iran . Nashville, Tennessee: Cumberland House Publishing, 2005, pg212, 213 and 214.

[127] Latifi, Afschineh. Even After All This Time: A Story of Love, Revolution, and Leaving Iran. NY, NY: Regan Books, 2005, pg15.

[128] Latifi, Afschineh. Even After All This Time: A Story of Love, Revolution, and Leaving Iran. NY, NY: Regan Books, 2005, pg14.

[129] Latifi, Afschineh. Even After All This Time: A Story of Love, Revolution, and Leaving Iran. NY, NY: Regan Books, 2005, pg16.

[130] Latifi, Afschineh. Even After All This Time: A Story of Love, Revolution, and Leaving Iran. NY, NY: Regan Books, 2005, pg16-17.

[131] Latifi, Afschineh. Even After All This Time: A Story of Love, Revolution, and Leaving Iran. NY, NY: Regan Books, 2005, pg69.

[132] Latifi, Afschineh. Even After All This Time: A Story of Love, Revolution, and Leaving Iran. NY, NY: Regan Books, 2005, pg302.

[133] http://wwwiranproject.info/articles/article.asp?Key=15

[134] http://wwwiranproject.info/articles/article.asp?Key=15

[135] http://wwwiranproject.info/articles/article.asp?Key=15

[136] http://www.iranian.ws/iran_news/publish/ 09th May 2006

[137] http://www.iranian.ws/iran_news/publish/ 09th May 2006

[138] Timmerman R. Kenneth. Countdown To Crisis: The Coming Nuclear Showdown with Iran. NY, NY: Random House Inc., 2005, pg 325.

[139] Brym Robert. New Society: Sociology for the 21st Century. T.O ON: Harcourt Brace, 1995, pg15.22.

[140] Babayan, Kathryn. Mystics, Monarchs, and Messiahs. Harvard University: Harvard University Press, 2002, pg441.

[141] Newman J. Andrew. Safavid Iran: Rebirth of a Persian Empire. NY, NY: I.B. Tauris & Co Ltd., 2006, pg 96.

[142] Babayan, Kathryn. Mystics, Monarchs, and Messiahs. Harvard University: Harvard University Press, 2002, pg442.

[143] McMenemy, John. The Language of Canadian. Waterloo, ON: Wilfrid Laurier University Press, 1995, pg 220.

[144] Timmerman R. Kenneth. Countdown To Crisis: The Coming Nuclear Showdown with Iran. NY, NY: Random House Inc., 2005, pg 327.

www.ingramcontent.com/pod-product-compliance
Lightning Source LLC
Chambersburg PA
CBHW060410290526

45791CB00002B/686